Praise for J. M. G. Le Clézio's *The Prospector*

Hypnotic and mythic ... Le Clézio brilliantly conveys the sublime and terrible beauty of life and its twin, death, in devastating evocations ... a remarkable work.   ALA *Booklist* (starred review)

A gentle portrayal of a man haunted by visions of his ideal childhood ... [Le Clézio's] writing is deeply evocative and descriptive.
Publishers Weekly

Praise for J. M. G. Le Clézio's *Desert*

- ❦ Finalist for the American Library Association 2010 Notable Books List
- ❦ Finalist for the American Literary Translators Association 2010 National Translation Award
- ❦ Finalist for the French-American Foundation and Florence Gould Foundation 23rd Annual Translation Prize

Desert *is a rich, sprawling, searching, poetic, provocative, broadly historic and demanding novel, which in all those ways displays the essence of Le Clézio.*   The New York Times Book Review

In Desert, *as in all of his books, J. M. G. Le Clézio finds new ways of writing about the intersection of man and place, in a way that manages to create an encompassing and empathetic humanism that doesn't depend on the overestimation of human beings.*

Adam Gopnik

This work contains magnificent images of a lost culture in the North African desert, contrasted with a depiction of Europe seen through the eyes of unwanted immigrants. The main character is a utopian antithesis to the ugliness and brutality of European society.

from the Nobel citation by the Swedish Academy

THE AFRICAN

*Also by J. M. G. Le Clézio in English
from Verba Mundi Books and
David R. Godine, Publisher*

THE PROSPECTOR
translated by Carol Marks

DESERT
translated by C. Dickson

THE AFRICAN

Translated from the French by C. Dickson

David R. Godine · Publisher
Boston

First published in 2013 by
David R. Godine · Publisher
Post Office Box 450
Jaffrey, New Hampshire 03452
WWW.GODINE.COM

Originally published in French in 2004 as *L'Africain*
by Mercure de France
Copyright © 2004 by J. M. G. Le Clézio
Translation copyright © 2013 by C. Dickson

Cet ouvrage publié dans le cadre du programme d'aide à la publication
bénéficie du soutien du Ministère des Affaires Etrangères et du
Service Culturel de l'Ambassade de France représenté aux Etats-Unis.

This work received support from the French Ministry of Foreign Affairs
and the Cultural Services of the French Embassy in the United States
through their publishing assistance program.

Endpapers: Full page and detail of "Afrique du N.O. Carte 54" (1931)
from Librarie Hachette, Paris, courtesy of The David Rumsey Map
Collection, www.davidrumsey.com.

LIBRARY OF CONGRESS CATALOGING-IN-PUBLICATION DATA

Le Clézio, J.-M. G. (Jean-Marie Gustave), 1940–
The African / by J.M.G. Le Clezio.
p.   cm.
ISBN-13 978-1-56792-460-2 (alk. paper)
ISBN-10 1-56792-460-3 (alk. paper)
1. Le Clézio, J.-M. G. (Jean-Marie Gustave), 1940—Childhood and
youth. 2. Authors, French—20th century—Biography.
3. Nigeria—Description and travel. I. Title.
PQ2672.E25Z46 2012
843'.914—dc23
[B]
2012005141

FIRST PRINTING
Printed in the United States of America

CONTENTS

LIST OF ILLUSTRATIONS

*The photographs and map are from
the author's personal archives.*

BANSO
MEDICAL AREA

EVERY HUMAN being is the product of a father and a mother. One might not accept them, might not love them, might have doubts about them. But they're there, with their faces, their attitudes, their mannerisms and their idiosyncrasies, their illusions, their hopes, the shape of their hands and of their toes, the color of their eyes and hair, their manner of speaking, their thoughts, probably their age at death, all of that has become part of us.

For a long time I dreamt that my mother was black. I'd made up a life story, a past for myself, so I could flee reality when I returned from Africa to this country, to this city where I didn't know anyone, where I'd become a stranger. Then when my father came back to live with us in France upon his retirement, I discovered that in fact it was he who was the African. It was hard for me to admit that. I had to go back in time, start all over again, try to understand. I wrote this little book in memory of that experience.

BODIES

I HAVE A FEW things to say about the face I was given at birth. First of all, I had to accept it. To say I didn't like it would make it seem more important than it was to me as a child. I didn't hate it, I ignored it, I avoided it. I didn't look at mirrors. I think years went by without my ever seeing it. I would avert my eyes in photographs, as if someone else had taken my place.

Around the age of eight, I went to live in Nigeria, West Africa, in a fairly remote region where – apart from my mother and father – there were no Europeans, and where, to the child I was, all of humanity was made up solely of the Ibo and the Yoruba people. In the cabin where we lived (there's a colonial tinge to the word cabin that might be offensive today, but it accurately describes the lodgings the British government provided for military doctors, a cement slab for the floor, four unplastered, cinder block walls, a roof of corrugated metal covered with leaves, no decorations, hammocks hanging from the walls to be used as beds and – the only concession to comfort – a shower connected with iron pipes to a reservoir on the roof

3

that was heated by the sun), in that cabin then, there were no mirrors, no pictures, nothing to remind us of the world we'd lived in up until then. A crucifix that my father had hung on the wall, but with no human representation. That's where I learned to forget. It seems to me that the erasing of my face, and of all the faces around me, dates back to the moment I entered that cabin in Ogoja.

Also dating back to that moment, or resulting directly from it, if you will, is the emergence of bodies. My body, my mother's body, my brother's body, the bodies of the young boys in the village with whom I played, the bodies of African women on the paths around the house or at the market by the river. Their stature, their heavy breasts, the shiny skin on their backs. The boys' penises, their pink, circumcised glands. Faces, no doubt, but like leather masks, hardened, stitched with scars, with ritual markings. Protuberant bellies, navels that looked as if a flat stone had been sewn under the skin. The smell of bodies too, the touch of them, the skin that was not rough, but warm and light, bristling with thousands of hairs. I recall a feeling of extreme closeness, of many bodies all around me, a feeling I had never known before, a feeling that was both new and familiar, one that ruled out fear.

In Africa, the immodesty of bodies was marvelous. It lent perspective, depth, it multiplied sensations, wove a human web around me. It fit in with the Ibo country, the meanderings of the Aiya River, the village huts,

4

their straw-colored roofs, their earth-colored walls. It shone out in those names that worked their way inside of me and meant much more than the names of places: Ogoja, Abakaliki, Enugu, Obudu, Baterik, Ogrude, Obubra. It permeated the great wall of the rain forest that stood around us on all sides.

When you're a child, you don't use words (and words don't get used). Back then I was a very long way from adjectives, from nouns. I was incapable of saying, or even thinking: admirable, immense, power. But I could feel it. How the trees with their straight trunks soared up toward the night sky clamped over me, enveloping – as if in a tunnel – the bloody gash of the laterite road leading from Ogoja to Obudu. How

acutely I perceived the naked bodies shining with sweat in the village clearings, the large silhouettes of women with children hanging on their hips, all of those things come together to form a coherent whole, free of lies.

I remember entering Obudu quite well: the road emerges from the shadows of the forest into the bright sunlight and leads straight into the village. My father stops the car, he and my mother have to talk to the officials. I am alone in the middle of the crowd, I'm not afraid. Hands are touching me, running along my arms, over my hair, around the brim of my hat. Among all the people milling around me, there is an old woman – well, I didn't know she was old. I assume it's her age that I remarked first because she was different from the naked children and the men and the women of Ogoja, dressed more or less in Western clothing. When my mother comes back (perhaps slightly uneasy about the gathering), I motion toward the woman, "What's wrong with her? Is she sick?" I remember asking my mother that question. The naked body of that woman, full of folds, of wrinkles, her skin sagging like an empty water pouch, her elongated, flaccid breasts hanging down on her stomach, her dull, cracked, grayish skin, it all seems strange to me, but at the same time true. How could I have ever imagined that woman as my grandmother? And I didn't feel pity, or horror, but rather love and interest, kindled by having glimpsed a truth, a real-life experience. All I can remember is that question, "Is she sick?" Strangely enough it still burns in my mind today, as if time had stood still. And not the answer – probably reassuring, perhaps a bit embarrassed – my mother gave, "No, she's not sick, she's just old." Old age, probably more shocking for a child to see on a woman's body, since ordinarily in France, in Europe – land of girdles and petticoats, of brassieres and slips – women are still exempt, as they've always been, from the disease of aging. I can still feel my cheeks burning, it goes hand in hand with the naïve question and my mother's brutal response, like a slap. All of that remained unanswered inside of me. The question probably wasn't: Why has that woman become deformed and worn with old age in that way? But rather: Why have I been lied to? Why has that truth been hidden from me?

Africa was more about bodies than faces. It was an explosion of sensations, of appetites, of seasons. The very first memory I have of that continent is my body being covered with little blisters caused by the extreme heat, a benign disorder that affects white people when they enter the equatorial zone, comically known as *bourbouille* – prickly heat in English. I'm in the cabin of the boat as it sails slowly down the coast past Conakry, Freetown, Monrovia, stretched out naked on the bunkbed, with the porthole hanging open to let in the humid air, my body sprinkled with talcum

powder. I feel as if I'm in an invisible sarcophagus, or as if I am a fish trapped in the boat, coated with flour, before being put into the frying pan. Africa was already taking my face away and giving me a painful, feverish body in return, the body that France had hidden from me in the anemic comfort of my grandmother's home, devoid of instinct, devoid of freedom.

In that boat bearing me away to another world, I was also being given a memory. The African present was erasing everything that had come before. The war, the confinement in the apartment in Nice (where in two attic rooms five of us lived, and sometimes even six, if you count the housemaid, Maria, whom my grandmother hadn't been able to resolve to let go), the rationing, or the flight into the mountains where my mother had to hide for fear of being rounded up by the Gestapo – all of that was fading away, disappearing, becoming unreal. From that moment on, there was to be a before and an after Africa for me.

Freedom in Ogoja was the supremacy of the body. Boundless, the view from the cement platform on which the house was built, like the cabin of a raft floating on the ocean of grass. If I search my memory, I can retrace the vague boundaries of our compound. Someone who had kept photographs of it would be surprised at the things a child of eight was able to see there. A garden, probably. Not a pleasure garden – did anything in that country exist for pleasure alone? But a useful one, where my father had planted an orchard: mango, guava, and papaya trees and, to serve as a hedge in front of the veranda, orange and lime trees, most of whose leaves had been stitched up by ants to make their suspended nests filled with a sort of cottony fluff that protected their eggs. Somewhere amid the bushes in back of the house, a coop where guinea fowl and chickens cohabited, the existence of which I was only aware of due to the presence – directly over it in the sky – of vultures that my father would sometimes shoot at with a rifle. All right then, a garden, since one of our servants was called a "garden boy." At the other end of the lot there must have been the cabins for the servants: the "boy," the "small boy," and especially, the cook, whom my mother was fond of, and with whom she concocted recipes, not traditional French food – but peanut soup, roasted potatoes or *foufou*, the yam paste that was our daily fare. Every once in a while, my mother would launch into experiments with him, guava jam or candied papaya, or even sherbet that she'd crank by hand. In that courtyard there were, most importantly, always lots of children who would come over to play and talk every morning and whom we didn't take leave of until nightfall.

All this might give one the impression of a very organized, colonial, almost urbane life – or at least a rustic one, in the manner of the English or the Normans before the industrial revolution. Nevertheless, it was absolute freedom of the body and mind. In front of the house, in the opposite direction from the hospital where my father worked, began an endless, slightly rolling, open stretch reaching out as far as the eye could see. To the south, the slope led down to the misty valley of the Aiya, an affluent of the Cross River, and to the villages Ogoja, Ijama, Bawop. To the north and the east, I could see the great wild plain scattered with giant termite mounds – cut off from the streams and the swamps – and the beginning of the forest, the stands of giants – irokos, okoumés – and, stretched over it all, an immense sky, a raw blue dome in which the sun burned down, invaded by storm clouds every afternoon.

I recall the violence of it all. Not the secret, hypocritical, terrifying violence that all children born in the middle of a war are familiar with – having to hide when I went out, spying on Germans in gray greatcoats while they stole the tires from my grandmother's De Dion-Bouton, listening again in a dream to stories of trafficking, of espionage, veiled words, messages that came from my father via Mr. Ogilvy, the American consular officer, and especially hunger, the lack of everything, the rumor about my grandmother's cousins eating only vegetable peelings. That violence wasn't actually physical. It was muted and hidden like an illness. It was eating away at my body, it gave me irrepressible fits of coughing, such painful migraines that I would hide under the long skirt of the side table, my fists pushed into my eye sockets.

Ogoja introduced me to another kind of violence, one that was open, real, that made my body tingle. It could be seen in every detail of life and nature all around. Thunderstorms, the likes of which I have never seen or dreamt of since, the inky sky streaked with lightning, the wind bending over the tall trees around our garden, ripping the palm leaves from the roof, slipping under the doors to whirl around the dining room and blow out the oil lamps. Some evenings, a red wind from the north that would set the walls aglow. Sheer electrical energy that I had to accept, grow accustomed to. To that end, my mother made up a game. Count the seconds separating us from the lightning's point of impact when we heard the first thunderclap, listen to it approaching kilometer after kilometer and then fading away out toward the mountains. One afternoon, my father was operating at the

hospital when the lightning burst in through the door and silently spread out over the floor, melting the metal legs of the operating table and burning the rubber soles of my father's sandals, then the bolt gathered itself back together and went out the way it had come, like an ectoplasm, to return to the depths of the sky. Reality was in the legends.

Africa was powerful. For the child I was, violence was all-pervasive, unequivocal. It filled us with enthusiasm. It's hard to talk about it today, after so many catastrophes, so much indifference. Few Europeans have experienced that feeling. The work my father carried out, first in Cameroon and later in Nigeria, created an exceptional situation. Most of the British with assignments in the colony accomplished administrative duties. They were military appointees, judges, district officers (or D.O.s, the British pronunciation of which made me think of a religious term, as if it were a variation on "Deo Gratias" from the mass my mother celebrated on our covered terrace every Sunday morning). My father was the only doctor within a sixty-kilometer radius. But citing that distance is meaningless: the first administrative city was Abakaliki, a four-hour drive, and to get there you had to cross the Aiya River on a raft, and then a dense forest. Another D.O. resided near the French Cameroon border, in Obudu, at the foot of the hills where gorillas still lived. In Ogoja, my father was manager of the dispensary (an old religious hospital the nuns had abandoned), and the only doctor north of the province of Cross River. He did everything there, as he later said, from delivering babies to performing autopsies. My brother and I were the only white children in the whole region. We hadn't the slightest inkling about what might forge the somewhat stereotyped identity of children brought up in "the colonies." When I read British "colonial" novels of those years, or the years just prior to our arrival in Nigeria – for example Joyce Cary, the author of *Mister Johnson* – they are completely unfamiliar to me. When I read William Boyd, who also spent part of his childhood in British West Africa, I can't relate to it either. His father was a D.O. (in Accra, Ghana, I believe). I never experienced what he describes – the cumbersome colonialism, the ridiculous antics of the expatriate white society on the coast, all of the pettiness that children take particular notice of, the disdain for the native people, of whom they knew only the faction of servants who had to indulge the whims of their masters' children, and above all, that sort of clique that both unifies and separates children of the same blood and in which they are able to glimpse an ironical reflection of their defects and their masquerades, and that, in a manner of speaking, forms the training ground for racial awareness that, in their case, takes the place of the school of human awareness. Thank God I can say all of that is completely foreign to me.

We didn't go to school. We didn't belong to any club, didn't practice any organized sports, didn't have any rules, or any friends in the sense that we use the word in France or in England. The memory I have of those days could be likened to time spent aboard a boat between two worlds. When I look at the only photograph I've kept of the house in Ogoja (a tiny snapshot, the standard 6 × 6 centimeter post-war format), it's hard for me to believe that it's the same place: a large open garden where palms and flamboyant trees grow haphazardly, traversed by a straight driveway where my father's monumental Ford V8 is parked. An ordinary house with a corrugated iron roof and, in the background, the first tall trees of the forest. There is something cold, almost austere about that unique snapshot, something that evokes the empire, an odd mixture of a military camp, a well-kept English lawn, and the forces of nature, something that I didn't encounter again until long afterward, in the Panama Canal Zone.

It was there, in that setting, that I lived the moments of my wild, free, almost dangerous life. A freedom of movement, of thought, and of emotions that I have never known since. Memories can probably be misleading. I must have only dreamt about that life of absolute freedom rather than having really lived it. Between the dreariness of the South of France during the war, and the bleak end of my childhood in Nice in the 1950s, rejected by my classmates because of my oddness, obsessed with my father's excessive authority, doomed to years in the Boy Scouts, to the extreme vulgarity of high school, then during my adolescence, to the menace of having to go to war to maintain the privileges of the last existing colonial society.

So the days in Ogoja had become my treasure, the luminous past that I could not lose. I recalled the blaze of light on the red earth, the sun that cracked the roads, the barefoot race through the savannah all the way out to the termite fortresses, the thunderstorm rising in the evening, the nights filled with sounds, with cries, our female cat making love with the *tigrillos* on the sheet metal roof, the torpor that set in after a fever, the cold coming in under the mosquito netting at dawn. All of that heat, that burning, that tingling.

TERMITES, ANTS, ETC.

IN FRONT OF the house in Ogoja, once you'd gone past the barrier around the garden (a wall of brush rather than a straight, neatly trimmed hedge), the great grassy plain that stretched all the way out to the Aiya River began. A child's memory exaggerates distances and heights. I have the impression that the plain was as vast as a sea. I would stand on the edge of the cement slab that served as a walkway around the cabin for hours, my gaze lost in that immensity, following the waves of wind over the grasses, fixing my eyes on the little dusty whirlwinds that danced here and there over the dry earth, scrutinizing the splotches of shade at the foot of the irokos. I really was on the deck of a ship. Our cabin was the boat, not only the cinder block walls and the sheet-metal roof, but everything that had to do with the British Empire – not unlike the *George Shotton*, a vessel I had heard about, an armored steamship equipped like a gunboat, topped with a roof of leaves where the British had set up the consular offices, that sailed up the Niger and

17

the Bénoué Rivers back in the days of Lord Lugard.

I was only a child, quite indifferent to the power of the empire, but my father followed its rules as if it alone gave meaning to life. He believed in discipline in the minutest acts of everyday life: rise early, make one's bed immediately, wash with cold water in the tin basin and save the water for soaking socks and underwear. My mother's lessons every morning, spelling, English, arithmetic, prayer time every evening, and curfew at nine o'clock. Nothing in common with the French style of upbringing, the games of "drop the handkerchief" and freeze tag, the joyful meals where everyone talks at the same time, and in the evening the *chante-fables* that my grandmother used to recite, daydreaming in bed, listening to the weather vane squeaking on the roof and to the adventures of a traveling magpie flying over the Norman countryside in the book entitled *The Joy of Reading*. In leaving for Africa, we had changed worlds. The freedom during the days compensated for the discipline in the mornings and evenings. The grassy plain in front of the house was immense, both dangerous and alluring like the sea.

I don't recall the day my brother and I first ventured out into the savannah. Maybe we were needled into it by the children in the village, an eclectic group including very small, completely naked toddlers with swollen bellies and near-adolescents of twelve or thirteen, dressed in khaki shorts and a shirt just as we were, and who had taught us to take off our shoes and wool socks to run barefoot through the grass. The same ones I see surrounding us in the rare photographs of that time, very dark-skinned, gangling, undoubtedly jeering roughnecks, but who had accepted us in spite of our differences.

In all probability, it was strictly forbidden. Since my father was gone all day, not to return until nightfall, we must have realized that applying the rules could only be relative. My mother was mild-mannered. She was undoubtedly busy with other things, reading, or writing inside the house to escape the afternoon heat. She had tried to become as African as she could. I suppose she must have thought there wasn't a safer place in the world for two boys of our age.

Was it hot? I can't recall in the least. I remember the cold in winter, in Nice, or in Roquebillière, I can still feel the freezing wind blowing through the narrow streets, cold as ice, as snow, in spite of our gaiters and sheepskin vests. But I don't remember being hot in Ogoja. When she saw us going out, my mother made us put on our Cawnpore helmets – in reality they were just straw hats that she had bought us before our departure in a shop in the old part of Nice. Among other rules imposed by my father was wearing wool socks and shiny leather shoes. As soon as he left for work, we took them off to run around barefoot. In the beginning, I wounded my feet running on the cement floor – I don't know why, I was always stubbing the big toe of my right foot. My mother would put a bandage on my foot, and I would hide it in my sock, and it would begin all over again.

Then one day, just the two of us went running over the straw-colored plain toward the river. The Aiya wasn't very wide in that particular place, but it rushed past with a mighty current, ripping clumps of red mud from the banks. The plain on either side of the river seemed endless. Here and there, in the middle of the savannah, stood tall trees with very straight trunks, which I later learned were used to supply mahogany floors to industrialized countries. There were also cotton plants and acacias that cast dappled shadows. We ran, almost without stopping, through the tall grasses that whipped our faces around the eyes, guided by the stems of the tall trees, until we lost our breath. Even today, when I see images of Africa – the vast parks of Serengeti or Kenya – I feel a thrill in my heart, it's as if I recognize that plain we ran over every day, in the afternoon heat, aimlessly, like wild animals.

In the middle of the plain, far enough away so that we could no longer see our cabin, there were castles. Along a barren, dry patch of ground, dark red ruins of walls, the tops of which were blackened by fire, like the ramparts of an ancient citadel. Here and there, jutting up along the walls, were towers whose pinnacles seemed to have been pecked away by birds, hacked at, burned by lightning. The great walls encompassed an area as vast as a city. The walls, the towers, were taller than we were. We were only children, but as I remember them, those walls must have been taller than an adult man, and some of the towers must have been over six and a half feet tall.

We knew it was the city of termites.

How did we know? Maybe through my father, or one of the boys from the village. But no one came out there with us. We learned how to demolish those walls. We must have started by throwing a few rocks, to test it out, to listen to the cavernous sound they made in hitting the termite mounds. Then we started hitting the walls, the tall towers, with sticks, to watch the powdery earth crumble, lay bare the galleries, the blind creatures that lived in them. The next day, the workers had plugged up the cracks, tried to rebuild their towers. We struck again, until our hands were aching, as if we were combating an invisible enemy. We didn't talk, we just kept pounding, letting out cries of rage, and new sections of walls went crumbling down. It was a game. Was it a game? We felt imbued with power. Today I don't think of it as a spoiled child's sadistic pastime – the gratuitous cruelty little boys sometimes enjoy meting out to defenseless life forms, tearing the legs off a beetle, crushing a toad in the door jam – but as if we were under some sort of spell that the open stretch of savannah, the proximity of the forest, the fury of the sky, and the thunderstorms had cast upon us. Or perhaps it was our way of throwing off our father's draconian authority, returning blow for blow with our sticks.

The village children were never with us when we went out to destroy the termite mounds. That insatiable desire to demolish would certainly have astonished them. They, who lived in a world in which termites were a fact of life, played a role in legends. The termite god had created the rivers in the beginning of the world, and it was he who was guardian of the water for the inhabitants of the earth. Why destroy his home? The gratuitousness of that violence would have made no sense to them: with the exception of game-playing, any form of activity was for earning money, getting a treat, hunting for something saleable or edible. The older boys took care of the younger ones, they were never alone, never left to fend for themselves. Games, discussions, and light work alternated with no specific schedule: they gathered dead wood and dried manure patties for fuel while out for a walk, they spent hours drawing water at the wells while they chatted, they played trictrac on the dusty ground, or sat in front of the door to my father's house gazing out into the distance, not waiting for anything. If they pilfered something, it had to be useful, a piece of cake, a box of matches, an old rusty plate. From time to time the "garden boy" got irritated and shooed them off, throwing stones, but a second later they were back again.

So we were wild, like young colonists, sure of our freedom, our impunity, with no responsibilities, no elders. When my father wasn't home, when my mother was asleep, we would escape, the straw-colored prairie would snatch us up. We went running as fast as we could, barefoot, far from the house, through the tall grasses that blinded us, jumping over rocks, on the dry, sun-crackled earth, all the way out to the termite cities. Our hearts were pounding, rage came spilling out with our heaving breaths, we picked up rocks, sticks, and we struck, struck, made great sections of those cathedrals topple, for no reason, simply for the pleasure of seeing the clouds of dust rise, hearing the towers come crashing down, the stick echoing on the hard walls, laying open to the light the red veins of the galleries seething with pallid, nacreous life. But perhaps in writing about it, I'm making the furor that ran through our arms as we struck at the termite mounds too literary, too symbolic. We were simply two children who had lived through the seclusion of five years of war, been brought up in a female environment, with a mixture of fear and cunning, where the only raised voice was that of my grandmother cursing the "Boches." Those days of running through the tall grasses in Ogoja were our first taste of freedom. The savannah, the thunderstorm that gathered every afternoon, the sun burning down on our heads, and that exaggerated, almost caricaturized presence of animality, that's what filled our small chests and threw us up against the great termite wall, those dark castles bristling against the sky. I don't think I've ever felt so driven since then. Such a strong urge to measure my strength, to dominate. It was a moment in our lives, just a moment, with no explanation, with no regrets, with no future, almost with no memory.

I thought it would have been different if we'd stayed in Ogoja, if we'd become just like the Africans. I would have learned to perceive, to sense things. Like the boys in the village, I would have learned to talk with living beings, discover the godliness in termites. I even think I would have forgotten about them after a while.

There was a feeling of haste, of urgency. We'd come from the far side of the earth (for Nice was truly another side of the world). From an apartment on the sixth floor of an upper-middle-class building ringed with a small garden where children were forbidden to play, we'd come to live in equatorial Africa on the banks of a muddy river in the middle of the forest. We didn't know we would ever leave there. Perhaps, like all children, we thought we would die there. Back there, across the sea, the world was mired in silence. A grandmother and her stories, a grandfather with his lilting Mauritian accent, playmates, classmates, it had all just stopped cold, like toys one puts away in a trunk, like the fears one shuts up in the closet. The grassy plain had obliterated it all, in the hot afternoon wind. The grassy plain had the power of making our hearts pound, of bringing forth the rage, of leaving us drained every evening, ready to drop into our hammocks.

* * *

The ants were the antithesis of that rage. The opposite of the grassy plain, of destructive violence. Were there ants prior to Ogoja? I don't remember them. Or most probably those "Argentinean ants" – black specks that would invade my grandmother's kitchen every night, along tiny routes leading from the potted rosebushes balanced on the gutter to the piles of refuse she burned in her boiler.

The ants in Ogoja were monstrous insects of the exsectoide strain that built their nests thirty feet under our lawn where hundreds of thousands of individuals lived. Contrary to the gentle, defenseless termites, incapable – in their blindness – of causing even the slightest harm, except that of consuming worm-eaten wood in houses and dead trees, the ants were fierce, red, with eyes and mandibles, able to secrete poison and attack whomever they encountered. They were the true rulers of Ogoja.

The bitter memory of my first encounter with the ants a few days after my arrival remains etched in my mind. I'm in the garden, not far from the house. I haven't noticed the crater marking the entrance to the anthill. All of a sudden, without realizing it, I'm surrounded by thousands of the creatures. Where are they coming from? I must have strayed into the bare area around the entrance to their galleries. It's not so much the ants that I recall, but the fear I feel. I stand there frozen, unable to flee, unable to think, suddenly the ground is seething, forming a carpet of armored bodies, of legs and antennae moving around me and swirling closer in on me, I see the ants climbing up on my shoes, working their way into the knit of those infamous wool socks my father made us wear. At the same time I feel the sting of the first bites on my ankles, along my legs. The dreadful, terrifying feeling of being eaten alive. It lasted a few seconds, a few minutes, as long as a nightmare. I don't remember, but I must have cried out, even screamed because the next minute my mother saves me, whisks me up in her arms and my brother, the neighbor boys are standing all around me in front of the terrace of the house, they are looking at me in silence, are they laughing? Are they saying, "Small boy him cry?" My mother takes off my socks, delicately turns them inside out, as one would peel off a dead skin, I see my legs – as if I'd been lashed with a thorny switch – covered with dark dots where drops of blood are forming, it's the ant heads clinging to the skin, their bodies had been ripped away when my mother pulled off my socks. Their mandibles are deeply embedded, they have to be taken out with a needle dipped in alcohol.

An anecdote, simply an anecdote. Why is it that I was so marked by it, as if the bites of the soldier ants were still painful, as if it had all happened yesterday? It's probably half legend, half dream. Before I was born, from what my mother tells me, she was traveling on horseback in Western Cameroon where my father was an itinerant doctor. At night they camped in "travelers' cabins," ordinary huts made of palm branches at the side of the road where they would hang their hammocks. One evening, the porters came to wake them up. They were carrying lit torches, they spoke in hushed voices, pressed my mother and father to get up. When my mother tells that story, she says the thing that alarmed her at first was the silence, everywhere all around in the forest, and the whispering of the porters. As soon as she was on her feet, she saw – by the light of the torches – a column of ants (those same red ants flanked by soldiers) coming out of the forest and starting into the cabin. A column, or more precisely, a thick uninterrupted river moving slowly forward, paying no heed to obstacles, moving straight ahead, each ant touching the one ahead of it, devouring, smashing everything along its way. My mother and father barely had time to gather up their belongings, their clothing, sacks of supplies and medicine. A second later, the dark river was flowing through the cabin.

How many times have I heard my mother tell that story? So many times I ended up believing it happened to me, confusing the ravenous river with the swarm of ants that attacked me. The churning movement of ants all around me is still there and I'm frozen in a dream, I listen to the silence, an acute, strident silence, more terrifying than any sound in the world. The silence of ants.

* * *

In Ogoja, there were insects everywhere. Day insects, night insects. Those that are repulsive to adults don't have the same effect on children. It's no strain of the imagination for me to conjure up again that nightly resurgence of armies of cockroaches – *cancrelats* – as my grandfather used to call them – the theme of one of those Mauritian riddles or *sirandanes* as they are called: *kankarla, nabit napas kilot,* cockroach got coat-tails, but got no drawers. They came out of the cracks in the floor, the planks of wood on the ceiling, they skittered around over by the kitchen. My father hated them. Every night, he'd roam around the house, flashlight in one hand, bedroom slipper in the other, for an endless and vain hunt. He was convinced that cockroaches were the cause of many diseases, even cancer. I remember hearing him say: "Brush your toenails well, or the cockroaches will come chew on them in the night!"

For us kids, they were just insects like all the others. We hunted and captured them, probably to release them near our parents' room. They were fat, brownish-red, very shiny. They took flight heavily.

We discovered other playmates: scorpions. Rarer than cockroaches, but we had a good-sized reserve. My father, who dreaded our rambunctiousness, set up two trapezes made of bits of rope and old tool handles on the side of the roofed terrace farthest from his room. We used the trapezes for a special exercise: hanging upside down by our knees, we would carefully lift the straw mat my father had put down to cushion an eventual fall, and watch the scorpions freeze in a defensive position, claws raised and tails brandishing their stingers. The scorpions that lived under the mat were generally small, black ones, probably inoffensive. But every so often, in the morning, they had been replaced by a larger specimen of a yellowish white color, and we knew instinctively it was a variety that could be particularly venomous. The game consisted in teasing those creatures from up on the trapezes with a blade of grass or a twig and watching them pace, as if magnetized, around the hand that was aggressing them. They never stung the instrument, their steely eyes could distinguish between the object and the hand that held it. Thus, to make things more interesting, we had to drop the twig every now and again and move our hand closer, then hastily withdraw it just as the scorpion's tail struck.

Today it's difficult for me to remember the feelings that motivated us. It seems that there was a good deal of respect involved in that ritual of the trapeze and the scorpions, respect that was obviously inspired by fear. Like the ants, the scorpions were the true inhabitants of the compound, we could be nothing more than unwanted and inevitable tenants, destined to leave some day. Colonists, in short.

One day the scorpions were the center of a dramatic scene that, whenever I think of it, still makes my heart race today. My father (it must have been on a Sunday

morning), had found a scorpion of the white variety in the cupboard. In fact, it was a female scorpion that was carrying her young on her back. My father could have squashed it with a slap of his dreaded slipper. But he didn't. He went to get a bottle of rubbing alcohol from his medicine cabinet, he poured some over the scorpion and struck a match. For some strange reason, the fire began burning around the creature, forming a ring of blue flames, and the female scorpion struck a tragic stance, claws lifted skyward, body tensed, raising the clearly visible venomous hook at the end of her tail over her children. A second squirt of alcohol engulfed her entirely in flames. The incident could not have lasted more than a few seconds, and yet I have the impression that I sat there watching her die for a long time. The female scorpion pivoted several times, her tail waving spasmodically. Her off-spring were already dead and fell shriveled from her back. Then she remained still, claws folded onto her chest in resignation, and the tall flames went out.

Every night, in a sort of revenge of the animal world, the cabin was invaded by myriads of flying insects. Some evenings, before the rain, there was an army of them. My father closed the doors and the shutters (there were no glass panes in the few windows we had), let down the mosquito netting over the beds and ham-mocks. It was a hopeless battle. In the dining room, we hurriedly ate our peanut soup in order to find shelter under the mosquito nets. The insects came in waves, we could hear them knocking up against the shutters, drawn by the light of the oil lamp. They came in through the cracks in the shutters, under the doors. They whirled crazily through the room, around the lamp, singeing themselves on the glass. On the walls, in the reflections of light, the geckos let out soft squeals each time they swallowed one of their prey. I don't know why, it seems to me that I've never had that close feeling of family, of being part of a unit, any-where else. After the burning day of running through the savannah, after the storm and its lightning, that stifling room was like the cabin of a boat closed up tight against the night, while the world of insects raged outside. In there, I was truly safe, like being inside a cave. The odor of peanut soup, of *foufou*, of cassava bread, my father's voice with its sing-songy accent relating anecdotes about his day at the hospital, and the feeling there was danger outside, the invisible host of moths batting against the shutters, the excited geckos, the hot, tense night, not a restful night of abandon like in the old days, but a feverish, trying night. And the taste of quinine in your mouth, that extraordinarily small and bitter pill you had to swallow with a glass of warm water dipped from the filter before bedtime to ward off malaria. Yes, I don't think I've ever again experienced such moments of intimacy, such a mingling of ritual and familiarity. So far from my grandmother's dining room, from the reassuring comfort of the old leather armchairs, of conversations that lulled one to sleep and of the steaming tureen, painted with a garland of holly.

THE AFRICAN

M Y FATHER came to Africa in 1928, after having served two years as an itinerant doctor on the rivers in British Guiana*. He left it in the early 1950s when the army decided he had passed retirement age and could no longer be of service. For more than twenty years he lived in the bush (a word that was used back then, but is no longer today), the only doctor in territories as large as entire countries, in which he was responsible for the health of thousands of people.

The man I met in 1948, the year I turned eight, was worn, prematurely aged by the equatorial climate. He'd become irritable due to the theophylline he took for his asthma, had grown bitter from loneliness, from having lived all the years of the war cut off from the rest of the world, not knowing what had become of his family, unable to leave his post to go to the aid of his wife and children or even to send them any money.

The greatest demonstration of love he showed for his family was when he crossed the desert in the middle

---

* On the northern coast of South America (1814–1966), now Guyana.

of the war to try and join his wife and children and bring them back to safety in Africa. He was stopped before he reached Algiers and had to return to Nigeria. It wasn't until the end of the war that he was able to see his wife again and meet his children during a brief visit which I have no memory of whatsoever. Those long years of silence and of living in remote places, during which he pursued his career of practicing medicine in emergency situations, with no equipment, no medicine, while people were killing each other all over the world, must have been extremely difficult, must have been unbearable, filled with desperation. He never spoke of it. He never intimated that anything in his life had been exceptional. All I was able to learn about that period was what my mother told me or sometimes allowed to slip out in a sigh: "Those were hard years, during the war, separated from one another . . ." Even then, she wasn't speaking of herself, she was referring to the anxiety of being a woman alone with two small children and no resources – trapped by the war. I imagine it must have been hard for many women in France, with their husbands imprisoned in Germany, or having disappeared without a trace. That is undoubtedly why that horrendous period seemed normal to me. There were no men, I was surrounded by nothing but women and very old people. It wasn't until long afterward, when the selfishness that is natural to children had worn off, that I understood: due to the war, my mother – in living far from my father – was an example of humble heroism, not through rashness or resignation (even though her religious faith had been of great succor to her), but through the strength that such inhumanity inspired in her.

Was it the war – that interminable silence – that had made my father into that pessimistic and cranky authoritative man whom we learned to fear rather than love? Was it Africa? Then which Africa? Certainly not the one we see today, in literature or in films, boisterous, unruly, juvenile, informal, with its villages run by matrons, its storytellers, the Africa in which one can constantly witness the admirable will to survive in conditions that would seem insurmountable to inhabitants of more privileged regions. That Africa already existed before the war, there's no doubt about that. I try to imagine Douala, Port Harcourt, the streets packed with cars, the markets where children gleaming with sweat run, groups of women talking in the shade of the trees. The large cities, Onitsha and its paperback book market, the rumbling of boats pushing logs upriver. Lagos, Ibadan, Cotonou, intermingling of all sorts, of people, of languages, the humorous, stereotypical side of colonial society, the businessmen dressed in suits and hats, impeccably folded umbrellas, the stifling salons where Englishwomen in low-cut dresses sit fanning themselves, the terraces of clubs where agents from Lloyd's, from Glyn Mills, from Barclays smoke their cigars, exchanging comments about the weather – It's a tough country, old chap – and the servants in tailcoats and white gloves silently make the rounds carrying cocktails on silver trays.

My father told me one day how he had decided to go to the other end of the world when he'd finished his medical studies at Saint Joseph's Hospital in Elephant and Castle, London. Since he'd received a government scholarship, he was expected to go to work for the community. He was therefore assigned to the tropical diseases ward at the Southampton Hospital. He takes the train, gets off at Southampton, rents a furnished room, a letter is awaiting him there, a very curt note from the head of the hospital saying, "Sir, I have yet to receive your calling card." My father has the cards in question printed up (I still have one of them), just his name, no address, no title. And he asks to be transferred to the Ministry of the Colonies. A few days later he's on board a boat heading for Georgetown, in Guiana. With the exception of a few short vacations, for his marriage and later for the birth of his children, he didn't return to Europe until the end of his professional career.

I tried to imagine what his life (and therefore mine) might have been if, instead of fleeing, he'd accepted the authority of the head of the Southampton Clinic and become a country doctor on the outskirts of London (just as my grandfather had been on the outskirts of Paris), in Richmond for example, or even in Scotland (a country he'd always loved). I don't mean to evoke the changes it might have meant for his children (for being born here or there isn't really of any importance in the end). But rather what it would have changed about the man himself, to have lived a more conventional, less solitary life. To have treated colds and constipation, rather than leprosy and malaria or lethargic encephalitis. To have learned to communicate, not in that singular fashion, with gestures, with interpreters, or in that rudimentary language known as pidgin English (nothing in common with the very refined, mystical Creole of Mauritius), but in everyday life, with completely ordinary people who make you one of them, who make you part of a city, of a neighborhood, of a community.

He had chosen something else altogether. Out of pride probably, to flee the mediocrity of British society, out of a desire for adventure too. And there was a price to pay for that something else. It plunged you into a different world, swept you away to another life. It condemned you to exile when war broke out, caused you to lose your wife and children, and in a certain way, inevitably made a stranger out of you.

The first time that I saw my father, in Ogoja, it seemed to me he was wearing a pince-nez. What makes me think that? The pince-nez was already rather old-fashioned in that day. Maybe a few old codgers in Nice had held on to that accessory, which – I believed – perfectly suited ex-officers of the Russian Imperial

Army sporting mustaches and sideburns, or else the type of bankrupt inventors who were friends of my "aunts." Why him? In reality, my father must have worn the type of glasses that were in style in the 1930s, steel-rimmed frames and round lenses that reflected the light. The same kind I see in portraits of men of his generation. Louis Jouvet or James Joyce (whom he slightly resembled for that matter). But an ordinary pair of glasses wasn't enough for the image of that first meeting that stuck in my mind, his oddness, the hard look in his eyes, emphasized by the two vertical creases between his eyebrows. The English, or rather British aura about him, the stiffness of his dress, a sort of rigid armor that he'd donned once and for all.

I believe that in the hours following my arrival in Nigeria – the long dirt road from Port Harcourt to Ogoja in the driving rain, sitting in the gigantic, futuristic Ford V8 that didn't resemble any other known vehicle – it wasn't Africa that had been a shock to me, but discovering that odd, unfamiliar, possibly dangerous father. Could my father, my *real* father have worn a pince-nez?

His authoritativeness immediately posed a problem. My brother and I had lived in a sort of blissful anarchy almost totally devoid of discipline. The little authority we'd been confronted with came from my grandmother, a refined and generous old lady who was fundamentally opposed to all forms of corporal punishment for children, preferring instead to employ reason and gentleness. During his childhood in Mauritius, my maternal grandfather had been raised with stricter principles, but his advanced age, the love he bore my grandmother, and that sort of phlegmatic aloofness peculiar to heavy smokers kept him shut away in a small cubbyhole in which he'd lock himself to be able to smoke his Caporal in peace.

As for my mother, she was full of imagination and charm. We loved her, and I suppose our mischievousness made her laugh. I don't remember having ever heard her raise her voice. Consequently, we had carte blanche to establish a reign of infantile terror in the small apartment. In the years that preceded our departure for Africa we did things that, with the hindsight of age, actually seem pretty awful to me: one day, goaded on by my brother, I scaled the railing of the balcony (I can still see it, quite a bit over my head) to climb up on the gutter overlooking the whole neighborhood from six floors up. I think my mother and grandparents were so frightened that – once we'd consented to come back in – they forgot to punish us.

I also remember being seized with temper tantrums because I'd been refused something, a sweet, a toy – in a word, for such trivial reasons I can't even remember them. I would be filled with so much anger I would throw whatever I could get my hands on out the window, even furniture. At times like that, nothing and no one could calm me down. Sometimes I can call up the feelings of those fits of rage, I believe it's something similar to being inebriated on ether (ether was given to children to inhale before extracting their tonsils). The complete loss of control, that feeling of floating, and at the same time of being extremely lucid. It was back in the days when I was also subject to violent headaches sometimes so unbearable that I had to hide under the furniture to escape the light. Where did those attacks come from? Today it seems to me that the only explanation would be the anxiety of the war years. A

closed, dark, hopeless world. The wretched food – the black bread that people said was mixed with sawdust, and that almost caused my death at the age of three. The bombing of the harbor in Nice that flung me to the floor of my grandmother's bathroom, that unforgettable feeling of the floor falling out from under my feet. Or still yet the ulcer on my grandmother's leg, which had grown worse with the shortages and the lack of medicine; I'm in the mountain village where my mother has gone to hide due to my father being in the British army and the risk of her being deported. We are standing in line in front of the food store and I'm watching the flies alighting on the open wound on my grandmother's leg.

The journey to Africa brought all of that to an end. One radical change: upon instructions from my father, before departing, I was to cut my hair – which I had worn long until then, after the fashion of young boys from Brittany – which resulted in my getting an extraordinarily bad case of sunburn on my ears, and my being forced to enter the ranks of male normality. Never again did I have those horrendous migraines, never again would I be able to give free reign to the temper tantrums of my early childhood. To me, arriving in Africa meant entering the antechamber of the adult world.

FROM GEORGETOWN
TO VICTORIA

A T THIRTY YEARS of age, my father left Southampton aboard a mixed cargo headed for Georgetown,
in British Guiana. The rare pictures of him at the time
depict a robust, athletic-looking man, elegantly dressed
in a suit, a stiff-collared shirt, tie, vest, black leather
shoes. It had been almost eight years since he'd left
Mauritius, after that fatal day in 1919 when his family
had been evicted from the house in which he was born.
In the small notebook where he'd jotted down the main
events of the last days spent at Moka, he wrote: "I have
only one desire now, to go far away from here and
never to return." British Guiana was in fact on the other
side of the world, diametrically opposite to Mauritius.

Did the tragedy of Moka justify his going to such a
remote place? At the time of his departure, he was
undoubtedly filled with such determination that it
remained with him all of his life. He couldn't be like
other people. He couldn't forget. He never spoke of
the events which had led to the dispersion of all of the

members of his family. Except every now and again, just to let out a burst of anger.

For seven years he studied in London, first in an engineering school, then in medical school. His family had been ruined, and he had to rely entirely on a government grant. He couldn't afford to fail. He specialized in tropical medicine. He already knew he wouldn't have the means to set himself up in a private practice. The episode of the calling card that the head doctor of the Southampton hospital had demanded was only a pretext for cutting off ties with European society.

At the time, the only pleasurable thing in his life was going to see his uncle in Paris, the passion he felt for his first cousin, my mother. The vacations he spent in France with them were an imaginary return to a past which no longer existed. My father was born in the same house as his uncle, they had grown up there each in turn, they were familiar with the same places, they had known the same secrets, the same hiding places, gone swimming in the same stream. My mother had never lived there (she was born in Milly), but she had always heard her father speak of it, it was part of her past, it felt like an inaccessible yet familiar dream to her (for back then, Mauritius was so far away, one could only dream of it). She and my father were united by that dream, they were drawn to one another as are exiles from an inaccessible land.

No matter. My father had decided to go away, he

would go away. The Colonial Office assigned him to be a doctor on the rivers of Guiana. As soon as he arrived, he chartered a pirogue with a roof of palm leaves, propelled by a long-axle Ford motor. Aboard his pirogue, in the company of his team, nurses, pilot, guide and interpreter, he sailed up the rivers: the Mazaruni, the Essequeibo, the Kupurung, the Demerara.

He took pictures. With his Leica Bellows camera, he collected black-and-white snapshots that depicted, better than any words, the remoteness of the post, the enthusiasm he felt at discovering the new world. Tropical nature was not new to him. In Mauritius, in the ravines under the bridge in Moka, the Terre-Rouge River was no different from what he found upstream on the rivers in Guiana. But that country was immense, it didn't belong to human beings quite yet. His pictures show loneliness, abnegation, the feeling of having reached the most distant shore in the world. From the wharf at Berbice he photographed the dark sheet of water over which a pirogue is gliding past a village of sheet metal scattered with scraggly trees. His house – a sort of chalet of planks on stilts, on the edge of an empty road, flanked by an absurd lone palm tree. Or else the city of Georgetown, silent and slumbering in the heat, white houses with shutters closed against the sun, encircled by those same palm trees, haunting emblems of the tropics.

The pictures my father liked to take were those that

showed the interior of the continent, the incredible power of the rapids his pirogue had to bypass, being hauled up on logs alongside the tiered rocks where the water cascades down between the dark walls of the forest on either bank.

Kaburi Falls, on the Mazaruni, the Kamakusa hospital, the wooden houses along the river, the shops of diamond hunters. A sudden calm on an arm of the Mazaruni, a sparkling mirror of water that sweeps you away into a dream. In the photo, the stem of the pirogue can be seen floating down the river. I look at it and can feel the wind, smell the water, despite the rumbling of the motor, I can hear the unbroken whirr of insects in the forest, can feel the anxiety springing from the coming of night. At the mouth of Rio Demerara, the hoists are loading Demerara sugar onto rusty cargo ships. And on a beach, where the wash comes rippling up to die, two Indian children gaze out at me, a small boy of around six and his sister hardly any older than he is, both with bellies distended from parasites, their black hair in a "bowl cut" just over their eyebrows like mine at their age. From his stay in Guiana, my father brought back only the memory of those two Indian children standing at the edge of the river, watching him, grimacing a little from the sun. And the images of a still wild world that he glimpsed along the rivers. A mysterious and fragile world ruled by sickness, fear, the violence of gold prospectors and treasure hunters, one in which the despairing chant of the vanishing Amerindian world could be heard. If they are still alive, what has become of that boy and girl? They must be very elderly, near the end of their lives.

Later, a long time afterward, I too traveled to the land of the Indians, along the rivers. I met similar children. The world had probably changed a lot, the rivers and forests weren't as pure as they were in my father's youth. Yet I thought I understood the sense of adventure he'd felt getting off the boat in the port of Georgetown. I too bought a pirogue, I navigated standing upright in the bow, my toes splayed to get a firmer grip on the edge of the boat, swinging the long perch in my hands, watching the cormorants taking flight before me, listening to the wind whistling in my ears and the echoing of the outboard motor sinking into the dense forest behind me. In examining the picture taken by my father in the front of the pirogue, I recognized the prow by its slightly squared snout, the coiled mooring rope laying crossways in the hull to serve as a bench from time to time, the *canalete* or Indian paddle with a triangular blade. And before me, at the far end of that wide "lane" of river, the two great black walls of the forest closing back in.

When I returned from the Indian territories, my father was already ill, locked into that obstinate silence of his. I remember the gleam in his eyes when I told him I'd spoken of him to the Indians, and that they had invited him to come back to the rivers, that in exchange for his knowledge and medicine, they would offer him a house and food for as long as he wanted. He'd smiled faintly, I think he said, "Ten years ago, I would have gone." It was too late, you can't go back in time, even in your dreams.

His life in Guiana had prepared my father for Africa. After all that time spent on the rivers, he couldn't go back to Europe – much less to Mauritius, the tiny country where he'd felt imprisoned amongst so many vain, egotistical people. A position had just been created in West Africa, in the strip of land that had been taken away from Germany and put under British mandate at the end of the First World War and that was made up of eastern Nigeria and western Cameroon. My father volunteered. Early in 1928 he found himself aboard a boat skirting the African coast heading for Victoria on the Bay of Biafra.

It is the same journey I took twenty years later with my mother and brother to join my father in Nigeria after the war. But he wasn't a child being swept along in the current of events. He was thirty-two at the time, a man hardened by two years of medical experience in the tropics of South America, a man familiar with death and disease, having lived with them – unprotected – every day, in emergency situations. His brother Eugène, who was a doctor in Africa before him, had most cer-

tainly informed him: the country he was headed for
was not easy. Nigeria was of course "pacified," occupied
by the British army. But it was a region in which war
was all-pervasive, the war of human beings against
one another, the war against poverty, the war against
abuse and corruption inherited from colonization,
especially the war against germs. In Calabar, in Cameroon, the enemy was no longer Aro Chuku and his
oracle, or the army of Fulanis and their long rifles from
Arabia. The enemies were called kwashiorkor, vibrio
bacteria, tapeworm, bilharzia, smallpox, amoebic
dysentery. Confronted with these enemies, my father
must have found his medical bag to be very lightweight.
Scalpel, surgical clamps, trephine, stethoscope, tourni-
quets, and a few basic tools, including the brass syringe
which he later used for giving me vaccinations. Antibi-
otics, cortisone didn't exist yet. Sulfonamides were
rare, his powders and unguents looked more like the
potions of a witchdoctor. Vaccinations were available
in very restricted quantities, for combating epidemics.
The territory that needed to be covered in order to
carry out the battle against disease was immense. In
comparison with what awaited my father in Africa, the
expeditions upriver in Guiana undoubtedly seemed
like mere outings to him. He was to remain twenty-
two years in West Africa, until his physical strength
began to decline. He would experience everything
there, from the enthusiasm of his beginnings to the
discovery of the great rivers, the Niger, the Bénoué, all

the way out as far as the Cameroon highlands. He would share love and adventure with his wife, traveling the mountain paths on horseback. Then later the loneliness and anxiety of war, till it wore on him, till it embittered his last moments, the feeling of having surpassed the limits of just one lifetime.

I wasn't able to understand all of that till much later, in going away – as he had – to travel in another land. I read it, not in the rare objects, the masks, statuettes, and several pieces of furniture he had brought back from the Ibo country and the Grassfields of Cameroon. Nor even in looking at the photographs he took the first few years after arriving in Africa. I found it out by rediscovering, by learning to better see the objects of everyday life that had always been with him, even during his retirement in France; those cups, plates of blue and white enameled metal made in Sweden, the aluminum flatware he'd eaten with all those years, the stacked lunch pails he used to eat out of while in the field staying in travelers' cabins. And all the other objects, marked, dented from the jolts, bearing the traces of torrential rains and that peculiar faded color caused by the equatorial sun, objects he had refused to get rid of and that were, in his eyes, worth more than any traditional knick-knack or souvenir. His wooden trunks with metal banding, whose hinges and locks he'd repainted several times and upon which I could still read the address of their final destination: General Hospital, Victoria, Cameroons. Aside from that luggage, worthy of a voyager in the days of Kipling or Jules Verne, there was the whole collection of tins of shoe polish and cakes of black soap, the oil lamps, the alcohol burners, and those large tins of Marie biscuits in which he stored his tea and his granulated sugar until the very end of his life. His tools, as well, the surgical instruments that he used in France as cooking utensils, carving the chicken with a scalpel and serving it with a clamp. And lastly, the furniture, not those classical monoxylous stools and thrones of primitive art. He preferred his old folding canvas and bamboo armchair to them, the one he'd carried from one travelers' cabin to the next over all the mountain tracks, and the little table with a rattan top that he used as a stand for his radio, with which he listened – up until the end of his life – to the BBC news every evening at seven o'clock: *Pom pom pom pom! British Broadcasting Corporation, here is the news!*

It was as if he had never left Africa. When he returned to France, he continued his work-a-day habits – up at 6 A.M., dressed (always in those khaki pants of his), shoes polished, hat on head, ready to go out shopping at the market (just as he used to go on the rounds at the hospital), home at 8 A.M. to cook the meal – as meticulously as he would carry out a surgical procedure. He had retained all of the fussy habits of an ex-military man. The man who had trained to be a doctor in remote countries – who had learned to be ambidextrous, able to operate on himself using a mirror or to stitch up his own hernia. The man with the calloused hands of a surgeon, who could saw through a bone or put a splint in place, who could make knots and splices – that man no longer used his energy and knowledge for anything but those minute unrewarding tasks that most people in retirement refuse to do: with equal application, he would wash the dishes, repair the broken floor tiles in his apartment, wash his clothing, darn his socks, build benches and shelves out of crate wood. Africa had left a mark on him that fit closely with the legacy of the spartan upbringing he'd received from his family in Mauritius. The Western-style clothing he donned every morning to go to market must have made him uncomfortable. As soon as he returned home, he would slip into a large blue shirt like the tunics the Haoussas of Cameroon wear and wouldn't take it off until bedtime. That is my perception of him at the end of his life. No longer the adventurer or the inflexible military man. But rather an old man out of his element, exiled from his life and his passion for medicine, a survivor.

* * *

For my father, Africa had begun when he landed on the Gold Coast, in Accra. A typical picture of the colonies: European travelers, dressed in white and wearing Cawnpore helmets being disembarked in a basket and taken to shore in a pirogue navigated by black people. That Africa wasn't terribly disorienting: it was the narrow band of land that followed the contours of the coast, from the tip of Senegal down to the Gulf of Guinea that everyone coming from the metropolises to do business and turn a quick profit was familiar with. A society that had, in less than half a century, structured itself into castes, reserved domains, taboos, privileges, abuses, and profits. Bankers, salesmen, civil or military administrators, judges, policemen, and gendarmes. All around them, in the large port cities, Lomé, Cotonou, Lagos, as in Georgetown in Guiana, a clean, luxurious zone had been created, with perfect lawns and golf courses, and palaces built of stucco or rare woods amid vast palm groves on the banks of an artificial lake, like the residence of the director of medical services in Lagos. A little farther out, the circle of the colonized with the complex framework described by Rudyard Kipling with regards to India and by Rider Haggard concerning East Africa. The servant echelon – that expandable buffer of intermediaries – clerks, lackeys, guard dogs, drudges (there's no dearth of words!), dressed in semi-European style, wearing shoes and carrying black umbrellas. Lastly, on the outer edges, there was the immense ocean of

Africans, who knew Westerners only through their orders or the almost unreal vision of a sleek black car roaring through their neighborhoods and villages in a cloud of dust, honking.

That was the image my father hated. He who had broken away from Mauritius and its colonial past, who made fun of plantation owners and their grand airs, who had fled the conformism of British society where a man's worth was measured by his calling card alone, he who had traveled the wild rivers of Guiana, who had bandaged, stitched-up, nursed the diamond hunters, the undernourished Indians, that man could only loathe the colonial world and its brazen injustice, its cocktail parties and neatly attired golfers, its servants, its fifteen-year-old ebony mistress-prostitutes brought in through the backdoor and its official wives puffing in the heat and taking their resentment out on their servants over a pair of gloves, some dusty furniture, or broken china.

Had he spoken of it? Where does that sensation of deep-rooted repulsion I have felt for the colonial system since my childhood stem from? I must have picked up a word, a thought about the ridiculous behavior of administrators such as the district officer of Abakaliki whom my father sometimes took me to see and who lived amongst his pack of Pekingese dogs that were fed filet of beef and biscuits, and given exclusively mineral water to drink. Or else the tales of Great White Hunters traveling in convoys on lion and elephant

hunts, sporting rifles with telescopic sights and explod-
ing bullets who, when they encountered my father in
those remote lands, took him for a safari organizer
and questioned him regarding the presence of wild
animals. My father would answer, "In the twenty years
I've been living here, I've never seen one, unless you're
talking about snakes and vultures." Or still yet, the
district officer posted at Obudu, on the Cameroon
border, who got a kick out of having me touch the
skulls of the gorillas he'd killed and showing me the
hills in back of his house claiming that in the evening
you could hear the thumping noises the apes made
beating upon their chests to provoke him. And above
all, the haunting image that still remains with me, the
column of black prisoners in chains, walking in time
along the road that led to the Abakaliki swimming
pool, flanked by policemen armed with rifles.

Perhaps it was the way my mother saw this continent, with eyes that were so very pure, yet at the same
time tarnished by the modern world. I can't recall
what she said to my brother and me, when she spoke
of the country where she'd lived with my father, the
place we would join him in one day. I only know that
when my mother decided to marry my father and to
go and live in Cameroon, her Parisian friends had
said to her, "What, with the savages?" and she, after
everything my father had told her, simply responded,
"They're no more savage than the people in Paris!"

After Lagos, Owerri, Abo, not far from the Niger River. My father was already far from the "civilized" zone. He contemplated equatorial African landscapes such as André Gide describes in his *Travels in the Congo* (more or less contemporary to my father's arrival in Nigeria): the expanse of the river – vast as an arm of the sea – where pirogues and paddle-wheel boats navigated and its affluents – the Ahoada River with its "sampans" equipped with palm leaf roofs, propelled with poles, and nearer to the coast, the Calabar River and the indentation of the village of Obukun, hacked out of the dense forest with the aid of machetes. Those were the first sights that met my father's eyes in the country where he was to pass the greater part of his professional life, the country that – out of necessity – he would be forced to adopt as his true country.

I can imagine how exalted he felt upon arriving in Victoria after the twenty-day journey. In the collection of snapshots taken by my father in Africa, there is one that particularly moves me because it is the only one he chose to have blown up and framed. It conveys the way he felt at the time, the impression of being at the beginning, on the threshold of Africa, in almost virgin territory. It shows the mouth of the river, in the place where the fresh water mixes with the sea. Victoria Bay follows a curve that ends in a finger of land where the palm trees are bent over from the sea breeze. The waves break on the black rocks and come rippling up to die on the beach. The sea spray, swept aloft on the wind, veils the trees of the forest, mingles with the mists rising from the river and the marshes. There is something mysterious and wild about it, despite the beach and the palm trees. In the foreground, very near the river bank, is the white cabin my father was lodged in when he arrived. It's no coincidence that to designate those houses that Africans reserved for travelers, my father used the very Mauritian term "camp." If that landscape lends itself to the term, if it also makes my heart race, it's because it could be in Mauritius, at Tamarin Bay, for example, or else at Cap Malheureux where my father used to go on excursions when he was a child. Perhaps he'd thought, upon his arrival, that he would find part of his lost innocence, the memories that circumstances had torn from his heart? How could it not have crossed his mind? It was the same red earth, the same sky, the same incessant wind from the sea, and everywhere, on the roads, in the villages, the same faces, the same children's laughter, the same carefree equanimity. The original land in a way, where time had gone backwards, had unraveled the threads of mistakes and betrayals.

* * *

That's why I can feel his impatience, the pressing desire to go into the backcountry to begin his work as a doctor. From Victoria, the trails led him across Mount Cameroon toward the high plateaus where he was to take up his post in Bamenda. It was there that he was to work for the first years, in a half-tumbled-down hospital, a dispensary founded by Irish nuns, dried mud walls and a roof of palm leaves. There that he was to pass the happiest years of his life.

His house was Forestry House, a real two-story wooden house, with a roof of leaves that my father would take the utmost care in rebuilding. Below, down in the valley, not far from the prisons, was the Haussa town with pisé ramparts and high gates, exactly as it was during the glorious era of the Adamawa. A little off to one side, the other African town, the market, the palace of the King of Bamenda, and the guest house for the district officer and other officers of Her Majesty's (they came only once, to decorate the King). A picture taken by my father, undoubtedly somewhat satirical, shows these officials of the British government, standing stiffly in their starched shorts and shirts, wearing helmets, calves sheathed in their woolen stockings, watching the parade of the King's warriors, in loincloths, heads decorated with fur and feathers, brandishing their *assegais*.

My father brought my mother to Bamenda after their marriage and Forestry House was their first home. They filled it with their furniture, the only furniture

they ever bought, which they took with them everywhere: tables, armchairs carved out of trunks of iroko,
decorated with the traditional sculpture of the high
plateaus of western Cameroon, leopards, monkeys,
antelopes. My father took a picture of their living room
in Forestry House, decorated in a very pronounced
"colonial" style: above the fireplace mantle (it gets cold
in Bamenda in winter) hangs a large shield made of
hippopotamus skin, along with two crossed spears.
They are probably objects left behind by the preced-
ing occupant of the house, for it doesn't look like the
kind of thing my father would go out in search of. The
carved furniture, on the other hand, came back to
France with him. I spent a large part of my childhood
and my adolescence surrounded by that furniture, sitting on the stools to read dictionaries. I played with
the ebony statues, the bronze hand bells, I used the
cowrie shells as jacks. To me, those things, the
sculpted wood and the masks hanging on the walls
weren't in the least exotic. They were my African side,
they were a prolongation of my life, and in a certain
way, an explanation of it. And before my life, they
spoke of the time when my father and mother had
lived over there, in that other world where they had
been happy. How can I explain it? I felt surprised, and
even indignant, when I found out, long afterward, that
objects of that sort could be bought and exhibited by
people that had never known anything about all of
that, for whom they meant nothing, and even worse,

for whom those masks, those statues and those thrones weren't living things, but dead skin that is often called "art".

During the first years of their marriage, my mother and father lived their life as lovers there, in Forestry House and on the roads of the Cameroon highlands, as far out as Banso. Traveling along with them were their employees: Njong the *chocra*, Chindefondi the interpreter, Philippus the head porter. Philippus was my mother's friend. He was a short man with inborn Herculean strength, capable of pushing aside a tree trunk to clear the road or of carrying loads no one could have even lifted. My mother said that several times he'd helped her cross flooding rivers, holding her up over his head above the water.

Also traveling with them were the inseparable companions that my father had adopted upon his arrival in Bamenda: James and Pegasus, the capricious and gentle horses with white stars on their foreheads. And his dog, named Polisson, a sort of gangly pointer that would trot out ahead on the paths, and lay down at his feet wherever he stopped, even when my father was to pose for an official photograph in the company of kings.

BANSO*

I N MARCH OF 1932, my mother and father left the
Forestry House residence in Bamenda and set up
house in the mountains, in Banso, where a hospital
was to be built. Banso was at the end of the laterite
road that was negotiable by car in all seasons. It was at
the frontier of what was known as "wild" country, the
last outpost where British authority was recognized.
My father was to be the only doctor, and the only
European, which did not displease him.

The territory he was in charge of was immense.
It stretched from the border with Cameroon under
French mandate in the southeast, all the way to the
limits of the Adamawa emirate to the north and
included the majority of chiefdoms and small king-
doms that escaped the direct authority of England
after the departure of the Germans: Kantu, Abong,
Nkom, Bum, Foumban, Bali. On the map he drew
himself, my father noted the distances, not in kilometers, but in hours or days of walking time. The details

* Kumbo today

63

noted down on the map reveal the true dimensions of that country, the reason he loved it: the river fords, the deep or tumultuous rivers, the mountainsides to be climbed, the bends in the paths, the descents into valleys that cannot be tackled on horseback, the impassable cliffs. On the maps he drew, the names make up a litany, they speak of walking in the hot sun, through the grassy plains or scaling laboriously up mountains amidst the clouds: Kengawmeri, Mbiami, Tanya, Ntim, Wapiri, Ntem, Wanté, Mbam, Mfo, Yang, Ngonkar, Ngom, Nbirka, Ngu, a thirty-two-hour walk, meaning five days at a rate of ten kilometers a day over difficult terrain. In addition to the stopovers in hamlets, the bivouacs, the treatments to be given, the vaccinations, the discussions (the notorious palavers) with local authorities, the complaints that needed to be listened to, and the travel log to keep up, the budget to watch, the medicines to be ordered from Lagos, the instructions to leave with the medical officers and the nurses in the dispensaries.

For more than fifteen years, this would be his country. Probably no one has ever reached a better understanding of it than he, no one has ever traveled, probed, endured it to the extent he did. Encountered every inhabitant, brought many of them into the world, accompanied others on their journey toward death. And especially, loved it, because – though he didn't speak of it, though he never related a single thing about it – the mark and the trace left by those hills and forests,

those pastures and the people he met there, remained deep within him all the way to the end of his life.

At the time he was traveling through the north-western province, maps were nonexistent. The only printed map in his possession was the German army's general staff map in the scale of one centimeter to three kilometers plotted by Moisel in 1913. With the exception of the major rivers, the Donga Kari – an affluent of the Bénoué – in the north and the Cross River in the south, and the two ancient fortified cities of Banyo and Kentu, the map is inaccurate. Abong, the northern-most village in my father's medical territory, located at more than a ten-day walk, is noted on the German army's map with a question mark. The districts of Kaka, of Mbembé were so far from the coastal zone it was as if they belonged to a different country. Most of the people who lived there had never seen Europeans, the most elderly had horrid memories of the occupa-tion of the German army, executions, child abduc-tions. This much was certain – they hadn't the slightest idea of what the colonial powers of England or France represented and had no inkling of the war that was being prepared on the other side of the world. They weren't remote or wild regions (as my father would, however, have qualified Nigeria, and, in particular, the forest surrounding Ogoja). On the contrary, they lay in a prosperous land, where fruit trees, yams, and millet were cultivated, where animals were bred. The king-doms were central to a puissant territory influenced by Islam coming from the northern empires of Kano, the emirates of Bornu, Agadez, and Adamawa, imported by Fulani itinerant peddlers and Haussa warriors. To the east was Koro and Borroro country, to the south the ancient culture of the Bamouns de Foumban founded on trading. They were master metal workers and even used a system of writing invented in 1900 by King Njoya. All things considered, European colonization had affected the region very little. Douala, Lagos, Victoria were light years from there. The mountainous peoples of Banso still lived as they always had, at a slow pace, in harmony with the sublime nature that surrounded them, cultivating the land and grazing their herds of longhorn cows.

The snapshots my father took with his Leica show the admiration he felt for that country. For example, the Nsungli near Nkor: a side of Africa that has nothing to do with the coastal zone where a stifling atmosphere pervades, where the vegetation is suffocating, almost menacing. Where the presence of the occupying forces of the French and British armies is even more oppressive.

This was a country of distant horizons, with vaster skies, with lands stretching out as far as the eye could see. My mother and father felt a sense of freedom they had never experienced anywhere else. They would follow the trails all day long, sometimes on foot, sometimes on horseback and stop in the evenings to sleep under a tree out in the open, or in a rudimentary camp like in Kwolu, on the road to Kishong, a simple hut of dried mud and leaves where they hung up their hammocks. In Ntumbo, on the plateau, they passed a herd that my father photographed with my mother in the foreground. They are at such a high altitude that the sky seems to be resting on the moon-shaped horns of the cows and veils the mountain peaks all around them. Despite the poor quality of the development, my

mother and father's happiness is tangible. On the back of a picture taken somewhere in the Grassfields region, in Mbembé country, depicting the landscape where they have just spent the night, my father writes with uncustomary grandiloquence: "The immensity one beholds in the background is that of the endless plain."

I can sense the emotion he felt crossing the high plateaus and the grassy plains, riding on the narrow paths that snaked up the mountainsides, discovering new panoramas every minute, the blue outlines of the peaks emerging from the clouds like mirages, bathed in the African light, the harsh blaze of noon, the softened glow of twilight when the red earth and the straw-colored grasses seem to be lit from within by a sacred fire.

They also learned to know the exhilaration of a strenuous life, the weariness that causes one's legs to wobble after a day of riding when the time comes to dismount and guide the horse by its tether over to the bottom of the ravines. The burn of the sun, the thirst that cannot be quenched, or the chill of the rivers that had to be forded mid-current, with the water reaching the horses' chests. My mother rode sidesaddle as she'd learned to do at riding school in Ermenonville. And such an uncomfortable position – the segregation of sexes that was still the rule in the prewar years was surely a bit ridiculous – paradoxically gives her an African appearance. Something nonchalant and graceful, yet at the same time something very ancient, evocative of biblical times, or perhaps of Tuareg caravans in which the women traveled across the desert in baskets hanging from the sides of the dromedaries.

Thus she accompanied my father, along with the suite of porters and the interpreter, on his medical rounds through the mountains in the west. They went

from camp to camp in villages whose names my
father would note down on his map: Nikom, Babungo,
Nji Nikom, Luakom Ndye, Ngi, Obukun. At times the
camps were more than precarious, in Kwaja in Kaka
country, they stayed in a hut of branches with no window in the middle of a banana plantation. It was so
humid in there that every morning they had to put
the sheets and blankets out to dry on the roof. They
would stay for one or two nights, sometimes for a
week. The drinking water was sour and purplish from
permanganate; they bathed in the stream, cooked
over a fire of twigs at the entrance to the hut. Nights in
the mountains south of the equator were cold, rustling,
filled with the clamor of wild cats and the barking of
mandrills. And yet it was neither the Africa of Tar-
tarin, nor even that of John Huston. It was rather the
Africa depicted in *African Farm*, a real Africa, densely
populated, wracked with disease and tribal wars. But
powerful and exhilarating as well, with its countless
children, its dances, the good humor and cheerful-
ness of the shepherds met along the paths.

For my mother and father, their days in Banso
were the days of youth, of adventure. The Africa they
encountered in the course of their marches was not
colonial Africa. In keeping with one of its principles,
the British administration left the traditional political
structure with its kings, its religious chiefs, its judges,
its castes and its privileges in place.

When they arrived in a village, they were welcomed

by the king's emissaries, invited to the palavers, and photographed with the court. In one of those portraits, my mother and father pose around King Memfoï, of Banso. According to tradition, the king is naked to the waist, sitting on his throne, with his fly whisk in hand. On either side of him stand my mother and father wearing worn clothing, dusty from the journey, my mother in her long skirt and walking shoes, my father in a shirt with rolled-up sleeves and his khaki pants that are too baggy and too short, held up by a belt that looks like a piece of twine. They are smiling, they are happy, fancy-free on that adventure. Behind the king, a wall of the palace can be seen, a simple dwelling of dried mud bricks with shiny bits of straw.

At times, in the course of their journey through the mountains, nights were brutal, burning, sexual. My mother speaks of the celebrations that suddenly burst forth in the villages, like in Babungo, in Nkom country, a four-day march from Banso. In the center of the village, the masked theater is prepared. The tom-tom players are seated under a banyan tree, they beat the drums and the call of the music echoes into the distance. The women begin to dance, they are completely naked, except for a string of beads around their waists. They move along one behind the other, bent forward, their feet stamping the ground in rhythm to the drums. The men remain standing. Some wear grass skirts, others bear the masks of the gods. The master of the jujus leads the ceremony.

It begins at sunset, around six o'clock, and lasts till dawn of the next day. My mother and father lie on their cots of canvas webbing under the mosquito net, listening to the tom-toms beating in an unbroken rhythm, with hardly a flutter, like the beating of a heart. They are in love. Africa, at once wild and very human, is their honeymoon night. The sun had burned their bodies throughout the day, they are filled with an all-powerful electrical force. In my imagination, they make love that night, to the rhythm of the drums vibrating in the ground, holding on to one another tightly in the darkness, their skin covered with sweat, inside the hut of mud and branches no larger than a chicken coop. Then they fall asleep at dawn in the cold breath of morning that stirs the curtain of the mosquito net, enlaced, no longer hearing the fading rhythm of the last tom-toms.

THE RAGE OF OGOJA

WHEN I TRY to understand what changed that man, the fracture that occurred in his life, I think of the war. There was before the war and after the war. Before, for my mother and father, were the high plateaus of West Cameroon, the gentle hills of Bamenda and Banso, Forestry House, the paths through the Grassfields and the mountains of Mbam and of the Mbembé, Kaka, and Shanti territories. All of that, not like a paradise – it had nothing to do with the gentle languor of the coast in Victoria, the luxurious residences and the idleness of the colonists – but like a treasure of humanity, something powerful and generous like blood pulsing through young arteries.

It might have seemed like happiness. It was during that time that my mother got pregnant twice. The Africans have a custom of saying that humans are not born on the day they come out of their mother's womb, but in the place and at the moment of their conception. I know nothing about my birth (which I suppose is true of all of us). But if I go inside of myself, if I turn my eyes inward, I am aware of that force, the bubbling of energy, the soup of molecules ready to come together to form a body. And, even before the instant of conception, everything that preceded it, that is in the memory of Africa. Not an ideal, diffuse memory: the image of the high plateaus, the villages, the faces of old men, the wide-eyed children wasting away with dysentery, the contact with all of those bodies, the smell of human skin, the muffled moans. Despite all of that, because of all of that, those images are images of happiness, of the fulfillment that brought me into the world.

That memory is linked to the places, to the lay of the highlands, to the mountain sky, to the lightness of the morning air. To the love they felt for their house, that hut of dried mud and leaves, the courtyard in which the women and children came to sit every day, on the bare ground, waiting for my father to begin consulting, give a diagnosis, a vaccination. To the friendship that brought them closer to the inhabitants.

I remember my father's assistant in Banso as if I'd known him myself, old Ahidjo, who grew to be his advisor and his friend. He took care of everything, the supplies, the itinerary through the remote regions, the relations with the village chiefs, the porters' salaries, the condition of the travelers' cabins. He accompanied him on the journeys in the beginning, but his advanced age and his state of health made it impossible for him to continue doing so. He wasn't paid for the work he did. No doubt he gained in prestige, in esteem: he was the medical officer's troubleshooter. It was thanks to him that my father was able to establish himself in the country, be accepted by everyone (including the witchdoctors with whom he was in direct competition), and practice medicine. During the twenty-some years he spent in West Africa, my father made only two lasting friends: Ahidjo and "Doctor" Jeffries, a district officer in Bamenda who had a passion for archeology and anthropology. Shortly before my father's departure, Jeffries did in fact finish his Ph.D. and was hired by the University of Johannesburg. He sent news from time to time, in the form of articles and brochures having to do with his discoveries, and also, once a year for Boxing Day, a package of guava fruit pastes from South Africa.

As for Ahidjo, he wrote to my father in France on a regular basis for years. In 1960 at the time of independence, Ahidjo asked my father his opinion on the question of incorporating the western kingdoms into Nigeria. My father answered that, considering the history of the region, he thought it was preferable that they be integrated into francophone Cameroon, which had the advantage of being a peaceful country. Time has proven him right.

Then the letters ceased and my father heard from the nuns in Bamenda that his old friend had died. Similarly, one year the package of guava pastes from South Africa didn't arrive for the first day of the year and we learned that Doctor Jeffries had passed away.

That was how my father's last ties with his adopted country were severed. All that was left was the meager pension that the Nigerian government had pledged to pay its former civil servants when independence was declared. But not long afterward, the pension stopped too, as if his past life had entirely vanished.

So it was the war that had broken my father's African dream. In 1938 my mother left Nigeria to return to France and give birth with her parents at her side. The brief leave of absence that my father took for the birth of his first child made it possible for him to join my mother in Brittany, where he remained until the summer of 1939. He took the boat back to Africa just before the war was declared. He took up his new post at Ogoja, in the province of Cross River. When war broke out, he knew it would put Europe to fire and sword again, as it had in 1914. Perhaps he hoped, as did many people in Europe, that the advance of the German army could be checked at the border, and that Brittany, lying the furthest west possible, would be spared.

When news of the invasion of France reached him in June of 1940, it was too late to act. In Brittany, my mother saw the German troops marching by under her windows in Pont-l'Abbé, while the radio was announcing that the enemy had been stopped at the Marne. The orders of the *Kommandantur* were irrevocable: anyone who was not a permanent resident of Brittany was to leave. Though she had barely recovered from childbirth, my mother had no choice but to go, first to Paris, then on to the free zone. No news could circulate. In Nigeria, my father knew only what was transmitted by the BBC. For him, isolated in the bush, Africa had become a trap. Thousands of miles away, somewhere on the roads crowded with people in flight, my mother was driving my grandmother's old De Dion, taking her mother and father and her two children, a one-year-old and an infant of three months, along with her. That was probably when my father made that crazy attempt to cross the desert to Algeria so he could get on a boat going to the south of France to save his wife and children and bring them back to Africa with him. Would my mother have agreed to follow him? She would have had to abandon her parents in the middle of the upheaval, when they were in no condition to withstand the ordeal, face the dangers along the return journey, risk being captured by the Germans or the Italians and possibly deported.

My father probably had no real plan. He threw himself into the venture without even thinking. He left for Kano, in the north of Nigeria, and bought his passage aboard a caravan of trucks that were crossing the Sahara. The war hadn't reached the desert yet. The merchants continued to transport salt, wool, wood, raw materials. The sea routes had become dangerous and the Sahara made it possible to keep goods circulating. For a medical officer of the British army traveling alone, the plan was audacious, insane. My father made his way northward, camped in the Hoggar near Tamanghasset (Fort-Laperrine at the time). He hadn't had time to prepare for the journey, bring medicine, provisions. He shared in the daily fare of the Tuaregs who accompanied the caravan, he drank the water from the oases, as they did, alkaline water that purged those not accustomed to it. He took pictures of the desert all along the way, in Zinder, in In Guezzam, in the Hoggar Mountains. He photographed the Tama-cheq inscriptions on stones, the nomadic camps, girls with their faces painted black, children. He spent several days at the In Guezzam fort, on the border of the French possessions in the Sahara. A few buildings made of pisé, over which the French flag flew, and at the side of the road, a stopped truck, perhaps the one he was traveling in. He reached Arak, on the other side of the desert. He might have reached Fort Mac-Mahon, near El Goléa. In times of war, all strangers are spies. In the end he was stopped and turned back.

After that setback, Africa no longer had the same taste of freedom for him. Bamenda, Banso, was the happy period, up in the highland sanctuary surrounded by giants on all sides, Mount Bambouta at 2,700 meters, Kodju at 2,000, Oku at 3,000. He'd thought he would never leave there. He'd dreamt of a perfect life, in which his children would grow up in that natural setting, would become, as he had, inhabitants of that land.

Ogoja, to which he had been condemned by the war, was an outpost of the British colony, a large village in a stifling basin on the Aiya River, encircled by the forest, cut off from Cameroon by an inaccessible mountain range. The hospital he was in charge of had existed for a long time, it was a large cement building with a sheet-metal roof housing an operating room, dormitories for the patients, and a team of nurses and midwives. Though it was still a bit primitive (it was an hour's drive from the coast after all), it was organized. The D.O. was not far away, Cross River – the province's large administrative center – was in Abakliki, which was accessible by a motorable road.

The government house he lived in was right next to the hospital. It wasn't a lovely wooden building like Forestry House in Bamenda, nor a rudimentary pisé and palm leaf hut like his home in Banso. It was a modern, rather ugly house, made out of cement blocks with a corrugated metal roof that turned it into an oven every afternoon – and that my father quickly covered with leaves to insulate it from the heat.

What was his life like during those long years of war, alone in that large, empty house, having no news of his children or the woman he loved?

He threw himself into his work as a doctor. The carefree, easy way of life in Cameroon didn't exist in Ogoja. Though he still consulted in the bush, it was not on horseback along the paths that wound through the mountains. He used his car (the Ford V8 that he bought from his predecessor, more of a truck than an automobile, the one that made such a strong impression on me when he came to pick us up as we were getting off the boat in Port Harcourt). He went to

neighboring villages, linked by laterite tracks, Ijama, Nyonnya, Bawop, Amachi, Baterik, Bakalung, out as far as Obudu in the foothills of the Cameroon Mountains. The contact he had with his patients was no longer the same. There were too many of them. At the hospital in Ogoja, he didn't have time to talk, to listen to the complaints of the families. The women and children weren't allowed into the courtyard of the hospital, lighting cooking fires there was against the rules. The patients were in dormitories, lying on real metal beds with starched, very white sheets, they probably suffered as much from anxiety as they did from their illnesses. When he walked into the room, my father could read fear in their eyes. The doctor was not the man who brought them the virtues of Western medicine and who could share his knowledge with the village elders. He was a stranger whose reputation had spread throughout the land, one who cut off arms and legs when gangrene had set in, and whose only cure was contained in the instrument that was both terrifying and ludicrous, a copper syringe equipped with a six-centimeter needle.

Then my father discovered – after all those years of having felt close to the Africans, like a relative, a friend – that the doctor was just another instrument of colonial power, no different from the policeman, the judge, or the soldier. How could it have been otherwise? Exercising medicine also meant having power over people, and medical supervision also meant political supervision. The British army knew that all too well: at the turn of the century, after years of fierce resistance, it had conquered the magic of the last Ibo warriors with the might of its arms and modern technology in the sanctuary of Aro Chuku, at less than a day's march from Ogoja. It is not easy to change entire populations when the change is made under duress. My father probably learned that lesson from being plunged into loneliness and isolation by the war. That knowledge must have deepened his feeling of failure, of pessimism. I remember his telling me once, at the end of his life, that if he could do it all over again, he wouldn't be a doctor, but a veterinarian, because only animals are able to accept their suffering.

There was also the violence. In Banso, in Bamenda, in the Cameroon Mountains, my father was under the charm of the African people's gentleness and sense of humor.* In Ogoja, everything was different. The country was troubled by tribal warfare, retributions, scores being settled between villages. The roads, the trails were not safe, one could not go out unarmed. The Ibos of Calabar resisted European penetration most vehemently of all. They were said to be Christians (it was even one of the arguments that France used for sup-

---

* The reputation of the gentleness of the people in the Banso region could hardly be generalized to the rest of west Cameroon. In a study devoted to the Wiya people of the Province of Bamenda, Doctor Jeffries reports atrocities committed during the war that has always pitted them against the Fulanis of Kishong: when the latter capture a Wiya, they slice off his ears and cut off both arms at the elbows and, sewing the palms of his hands together, make a sort of collar that they put around the neck of the prisoner before sending him back to his village. The French and British occupying armies tried in vain to counter such exactions that are reappearing in certain countries in West Africa such as Liberia.

porting their struggle against their Yoruba neighbors, who were Muslims). In truth, animism and fetishism were common at the time. Witchcraft was also practiced in Cameroon, but for my father it was more straightforward, more positive. In eastern Nigeria witchcraft was secretive, it was practiced through the use of poisons, hidden amulets, signs intended to bring misfortune. My father heard for the very first time, from the mouths of the European residents and later spread around by the locals in their service, stories of possession, of magic, of ritual crimes. The legend of Aro Chuku and its human sacrifice stone still deeply affected people. The stories that went around created a climate of suspicion, of tension. In such and such a village, they say, not far from Obudu, the inhabitants have a custom of stretching a rope across the road when a lone traveler ventures out on a bicycle. As soon as he falls, the poor man is immediately clubbed over the head, dragged behind a wall and his body cut up to be eaten. In yet another village, the district officer confiscated what was purportedly pork from the butcher shop, but, as rumor has it, was in fact human flesh. In Obudu, where the gorillas from the mountains are poached, their amputated hands can be found on sale in the market as souvenirs, but they say that if you look more closely, you can see there are also children's hands for sale.

My father repeated those alarming stories to us, he

probably only half-believed them. He never saw any evidence of cannibalism himself. But one thing is certain: he often had to travel in order to autopsy murder victims. It was that kind of violence that haunted him. I heard my father say that the bodies he had to examine were sometimes in such a state of decomposition that he needed to tie the scalpel to the end of a piece of wood before cutting into the skin to avoid the explosion of gases.

To him there was something offensive about disease, once the charm of Africa had worn off. The profession he had exercised with enthusiasm gradually grew to be toilsome, in the heat, the humidity of the river, the solitude in that remote corner of the world. The close contact with suffering wore on him: all those bodies burning with fever, the bloated bellies of cancer patients, those legs eaten away with ulcers, deformed by elephantiasis, those faces gnawed away by leprosy or syphilis, those women torn apart in childbirth, those children grown old from deficiencies, their gray skin like parchment, their rust-colored hair, their eyes enlarged at their approaching death. A long time afterward, he talked to me about the terrible things he had to face, as if the same sequence of events would begin all over again every day: an old woman driven mad with uremia who must be tied to her bed, a man from whom he removes a tapeworm so long he has to wrap it around a stick, a young woman he is going to amputate due to gangrene, another one who is brought to him dying of smallpox, her face swollen and covered with pustules. Close physical contact with that land, the feeling one gets only from encountering humanity in all of its painful reality, the odor of skin, of sweat, of blood, the pain, the hope, the small gleam of light that sometimes illuminates a patient's gaze when the fever goes down, or that infinite second during which a doctor can see life burning out in a dying man's eye – all of that, everything that had inspired, had stimulated him in the beginning, when he sailed up the rivers in Guiana, when he walked the mountain paths in the Cameroon highlands, was put into question in Ogoja, because of the appalling grind of days filled with unexpressed pessimism, because he realized the impossibility of succeeding at his task.

His voice still husky with emotion, he told me about the young Ibo who was brought to the hospital in Ogoja, hands and feet bound, mouth gagged with a sort of wooden muzzle. He's been bitten by a dog and rabies has set in. He is lucid, he knows he is going to die. At times in the cell where he's been isolated, he is seized with attacks, his body arches up on the bed in spite of the ties, his limbs are possessed of such strength that the leather thongs seem to be near breaking. At the same time, he moans and screams in pain, foams at the mouth. Then he falls back into a sort of lethargy, numbed with morphine. A few hours later, my father inserts the needle that will carry the poison into his vein. Before dying the boy looks at my father, he loses consciousness and his chest collapses in one last sigh. What kind of man are you when you've lived through that?

NEGLECT

Such was the man I met in 1948, at the end of his African life. I didn't recognize him, didn't understand him. He was too different from everyone I knew, a stranger, and even more than that, almost an enemy. He had nothing in common with the men I had known in France in my grandmother's circle of acquaintances, those "uncles," my grandfather's friends, gentlemen of another age, distinguished, decorated, patriotic, revanchist, talkative, bearing gifts, having families, relations, subscribers to *The Travel Journal*, readers of Léon Daudet and Barrès. Always impeccably dressed in their gray suits, their vests, wearing stiff collars and ties, sporting their felt hats and wielding their metal-tipped walking sticks. After dinner, they would settle into the leather armchairs – souvenirs of prosperous times – in the dining room, they would smoke and talk, and I would fall asleep with my nose in my empty plate listening to the murmur of their voices.

The man that appeared before me at the foot of the gangway on the wharf at Port Harbor was from another world: wearing a shapeless pair of pants that were too baggy and too short for him, a white shirt, his black leather shoes dusty from the dirt tracks. He was harsh, taciturn. When he spoke French it was with the sing-song accent of Mauritius, or else he spoke in pidgin, that mysterious dialect that jingled like bells. He was inflexible, authoritative, yet at the same time gentle and generous with the Africans that worked for him at the hospital and in his government house. He was full of idiosyncrasies and conventions that were foreign to me, about which I hadn't the slightest inkling: children should never speak at the table without being authorized, they should not run, or play, or laze in bed. They could not eat between meals, and never eat sweet things. They should eat without laying their hands on the table, could not leave anything in their plates and should be careful never to chew with their mouths open. His obsession with hygiene led him to do amazing things, like washing his hands with alcohol and then lighting a match to them. He was forever verifying the charcoal in the water filter, drank nothing but tea, or even hot water (that the Chinese call white tea), made his own candles out of wax and bits of twine dipped in paraffin, washed the dishes himself with extracts of soapwort. With the exception of his radio connected to an antenna hanging across the garden, he had no contact with the rest of the world, read neither books nor newspapers. The only thing he read was a small black book that I found a long time afterward, and that I can't open without being moved: *The Imitation of Christ*, a military-man's book, as I presume soldiers in the past might have read *Meditations* by Marcus Aurelius on the battle-field. Of course, he never said anything to us about it.

As soon as we met him, my brother and I tested him by putting pepper in his teapot. That did not make him laugh, he chased us around the house and beat us soundly. Perhaps a different man, I mean one of those "uncles" that visited my grandmother's apart-ment, would have merely laughed. We suddenly learned that a father could be fearsome, that he could be ruth-less, go out and cut down switches in the woods to thrash our legs with. That he could establish a virile code of justice, ruling out all dialogue, all excuses. That the code was founded on example, refused all negotiations, all denunciations, the whole act of tears and promises we were used to bringing into play with my grandmother. That he would not tolerate the slightest manifestation of disrespect and would accept no propensity for tantrums: to me the matter was clear, the house in Ogoja was on one level, and there was no furniture or windows to throw it out of.

It was that same man who insisted on prayers being said every evening before bed, and Sundays being devoted to reading the mass book. The religion we discovered under his care did not allow for com-promises. It was a rule of life, a code of conduct. I sup-pose it was upon our arrival in Ogoja that we learned Santa Claus didn't exist, that ceremonies and religious holidays were reduced to prayers, and that there was no reason to offer presents that, in the context we were in, could only be superfluous.

Things would undoubtedly have been different if there hadn't been that fracture caused by the war, if my father, instead of being faced with children who had become strangers to him, had learned to live in the same house with a baby, if he had been part of the slow process that leads from childhood to the age of reason. That African land in which he had known the happiness of sharing his adventurous life with a woman, in Banso, in Bamenda, was the very same land that had robbed him of a family life and the love of his children.

Today I am able to feel regret at having missed that opportunity. I try to imagine what it must have meant for a child of eight, having grown up in the confinement of the war, to go to the other side of the world to meet a stranger who was introduced to him as his father. And that it should occur there, in Ogoja, in a natural setting where everything was excessive, the sun, the thunderstorms, the rain, the vegetation, the insects, a land of both freedom and constraint. Where the women and men were completely different, not because of the color of their skin and hair, but in their way of speaking, of walking, of laughing, of eating. Where disease and old age were visible, where joy and children's games were even more marked. Where

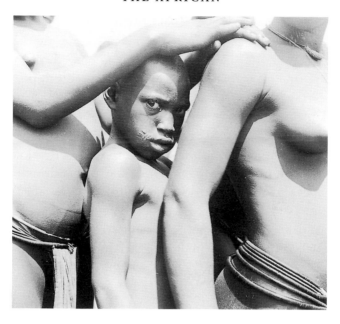

childhood ends very early, almost without transition,
where the boys work with their fathers, the little girls
get married and bear children of their own at thirteen.

It would have taken growing up listening to a father
telling about his life, singing songs, taking his sons out
to the River Aiya to hunt lizards or catch crayfish, it
would have taken slipping my hand into his so that he
could point out rare butterflies, venomous flowers, the
secrets of nature he must surely have known about,
listening to him talk about his childhood in Mauritius,
walking beside him when he went to visit his friends,

his colleagues at the hospital, watching him repair the car, or change a broken shutter, helping him plant the bushes and the flowers he loved, the bougainvilleas, the strelitzias, the birds-of-paradise, everything that must have reminded him of the marvelous garden of Moka, the house where he was born.

Instead, we waged a perfidious, grueling war against him, sparked by punishments and beatings. The period when he came back from Africa was the hardest. In addition to the difficulties he had in adapting, there was the hostility he must have felt in his own home. His fits of anger were disproportionate, excessive, exhausting. For insignificant things, a broken bowl, an inappropriate word, or look, he would mete out blows with the cane, with his fists. I remember having felt something akin to hatred. All I could do was break his sticks, but he went out and cut down others in the hills. There was something archaic about that approach, it didn't fit in with what my friends experienced. I must have come out hardened, as the Arab proverb goes: he who is beaten is weak at first, then he grows strong.

Today, in hindsight, I understand that my father was transmitting the most difficult part of an upbringing to us – that which no school will ever provide. Africa hadn't transformed him. It had brought out rigor in him. Later, when my father came to spend his retirement in the South of France, he brought that African heritage back with him. Authority and discipline, to the point of brutality.

But also exactness and respect, like one of the rules of the ancient societies of Cameroon and Nigeria, where children must not cry, must not complain. A penchant for a religion with no frills, no superstitions, that I suppose he developed using Islam as a model. That is how I have come to understand what seemed absurd back then, his obsession with hygiene, the way he washed his hands. The aversion he showed for pork, extracting the encysted tapeworm eggs from the meat with the tip of his knife, in order to convince us. His way of eating, of cooking his rice African-style, adding hot water little by little. His love of boiled vegetables, which he seasoned with hot pepper sauce. His preference for dried fruits, dates, figs, and even bananas that he would set out to dry in the sun on his windowsill. The care he took to go to the market very early every morning, in the company of North African laborers whom he also encountered at the police station every time he renewed his residence permit.

All of that might sound anecdotal. But those African habits, which had become second nature to him, surely brought home a lesson that could not leave a child or – later on – an adolescent indifferent.

Twenty-two years in Africa had inspired in him a deep hatred of all forms of colonialism. In 1954, we took a trip to Morocco (where one of the "uncles" was manager of an agricultural domain). I recall an incident that marked me much more than any of the traditional folklore. We had taken a regular bus from Casablanca to Marrakesh. At one point the driver (a Frenchman) grew angry, insulted an old peasant who probably could not pay the fare and threw him out on the side of the road. My father was indignant. His tirade extended out to include the entire French occupation of the country that prevented local people from holding the most menial of jobs, even that of a bus driver, and mistreated the poor. Around that same time, day after day, he would listen to the news on the radio about the Kikuyus' struggle for independence in Kenya and that of the Zulus against racial segregation in South Africa.

It had nothing to do with abstract ideas or political leanings. It was the voice of Africa that spoke within him, that awakened his earlier sentiments. He'd undoubtedly thought about the future when he was traveling with my mother on horseback along the trails in Cameroon. It was before the war, before the solitude and the bitterness, when everything was possible, when the country was young and new, when anything could happen. Far from the corrupt, profiteering society on the coast, he had dreamt of the rebirth of Africa, liberated from its colonial shackles and the inevitability of pandemics. A sort of state of grace, like that of the vast grassy expanses through which the herds moved driven by their shepherds, or the villages around Banso, with the immemorial perfection of their walls of pisé and their leaf-covered roofs.

The advent of independence in Cameroon and in

Nigeria, then – step by step – across the continent, must have impassioned him. Each insurrection must have been a source of joy for him. And the war which had just broken out in Algeria, a war his own children could have been drafted into, could only have been the worst of his nightmares. He'd never forgiven de Gaulle's double-dealing.

He died the year AIDS was discovered. He had already perceived the tactical state of neglect in which the colonial powers left the continent they had exploited. Tyrants were put into place with the aid of France and England – Bokassa, Idi Amin Dada – to whom the Western governments provided arms and subsidies for years, before repudiating them. The doors of immigration having been flung open, cohorts of young men left Ghana, Benin, or Nigeria during the sixties to serve as a labor force and populate the ghettos of the urban outskirts, then those same doors clamped shut again when the economic crisis made the industrial nations wary and xenophobic. And above all Africa was abandoned to its old demons, malaria, dysentery, famine. Now AIDS, the new plague, threatens a third of its general population with death, and again the Western countries, who control the remedies, pretend to see nothing, know nothing.

Cameroon, it seemed, had escaped those maledictions. The highlands of the west, in separating from Nigeria, had made a sensible decision, which protected the region from the corruption of tribal warfare. But the arrival of modernity did not bring the expected benefits. What had disappeared, in my father's eyes, was the charm of the villages, the slow, carefree life punctuated by the rhythm of agricultural tasks. The lure of money, venality, a certain degree of violence had replaced all of that. Even far from Banso, my father must have been aware of it. He must have felt the passing of time like an ebbing flow, leaving the tidemarks of memory behind.

In 1968, as my mother and father were observing the mountains of garbage left by the general strike piling up under their windows in Nice, and as I, in Mexico, was listening to the whirr of army helicopters carrying away the bodies of students killed in Tlatelolco, Nigeria was entering the last phase of a terrible massacre, one of the great genocides of the century, known by the name of Biafra. To gain control of the oil wells at the mouth of the Calabar River, Ibos and Yorubas were exterminating one another, as the Western world looked on with indifference. Worse yet, the large oil companies, mainly the Royal Dutch Shell and British Petroleum group, took sides in the war, putting pressure on their own governments to safeguard the wells and pipelines. The countries they represented confronted one another by proxy, France on the side of the Biafran insurgents, the Soviet Union, England, and the United States on the side of the federal government made up of a Yoruba majority. The civil war became a world issue, a war of civilizations. There was talk of Christians against Muslims, or of nationalists against capitalists. Developed countries discovered an unforeseen market for their manufactured products: to both sides they sold light and heavy weaponry, antipersonnel mines, combat tanks, planes, and even German, French, Chadian mercenaries who made up the Fourth Biafran Brigade serving the rebels in Ojukwu. But at the end of the summer of 1968, surrounded, decimated by the federal troops under the command of general Benjamin Adekunle, nicknamed the "Black Scorpion" for his cruelty, the Biafran army capitulated. Only a handful of combatants continued to resist, most of them children wielding machetes and sticks carved in the shape of rifles against Migs and Soviet bombers. At the fall of Aba (not far from the ancient sanctuary of the magician warriors of Aro Chuku), Biafra entered a long period of agony. In collusion with England and the United States, General Adekunle clamped down a blockade over the Biafran territory, preventing the arrival of all aid, all supplies. Before the advancing federal army in the grips of a mad desire for revenge, the population fled toward what was left of Biafra, flooding through the savannahs and the forest, trying to survive on their reserves. Men, women, children were caught in a deathtrap. From September onward, there were no more military operations, but millions of people were cut off from the rest of the world, without food, without medicine. When international organizations were finally able to penetrate the zone of the insurgency, they discovered the extent of the horror. Along the roads, on the banks of the rivers, at the entrances to villages, hundreds of thousands of children were dying of hunger or dehydration. It was a cemetery as vast as a country. Everywhere, in the grassy plains similar to the one where I once ran to wage war on the termites, children without parents wandered aimlessly, bodies transformed into skeletons. For a long time after that, I was haunted by Chinua Achebe's poem, "Christmas in Biafra," that begins with these words:

> *No, no Madonna and Child can match*
> *The picture of a mother's tenderness*
> *Toward the son she must soon forget.*

I saw the unbearable pictures in all of the newspapers. For the first time, the country in which I'd spent the most memorable period of my childhood was being shown to the rest of the world, but only because it was dying. My father also saw those pictures, how had he been able to accept it? At seventy-two years of age, one can only look on in silence. No doubt shed some tears.

The same year that the country he had lived in was destroyed, my father had his British citizenship revoked, due to the independence of the Isle of Mauritius. From that moment on, he stopped dreaming of going away. He had planned on going back to Africa, not to Cameroon, but to Durban in South Africa, to be closer to his brothers and sisters who had remained in Mauritius, where they were born. Then he had toyed with the idea of settling in the Bahamas, buying a plot of land in Eleuthera and building a sort of camp on it. He had pored over the maps. He was looking for a different place, not the ones he had known and suffered in, but a new world, where he could begin all over again, as if on an island. After the Biafran massacre, he dreamt no longer. He fell into a kind of obstinate silence that hung over him till his death. He even forgot he was a doctor who had led an adventurous, heroic life. After a bad case of flu, when he was briefly hospitalized for a blood transfusion, I had a difficult time having the results of his tests given to him. "Why do you want them?" asked the nurse, "Are you a doctor?" I answered, "Not me. But he is." The nurse brought the documents to him. "But why didn't you say you were a doctor?" My father responded, "Because you didn't ask me." In a way, I don't think it was really resignation, but rather a desire to identify with all the people he had treated, whom he began to resemble at the end of his life.

* * *

I am forever yearning to go back to Africa, to my childhood memory. To the source of my feelings, to that which molded my character. The world changes, it's true, and the boy who is standing over there on the plain amidst the tall grasses in the hot breath of wind bearing the odors of the savannah, the shrill sound of the forest, the boy feeling the dampness of the sky and the clouds upon his lips, that boy is so far from me that no story, no journey will ever make it possible for me to reach him again.

Yet, at times I walk aimlessly through the narrow streets of a town and suddenly, as I go past a door at the foot of a building under construction, I breathe in the cold smell of cement that has just been poured, and I'm back in the visitors' cabin at Abakaliki, I go into the shadowy cubicle of my room and see, behind the door, the big blue lizard that our cat strangled and brought to me as a sign of welcome. Or else, just when I'm least expecting it, I am submerged in the fragrance of wet earth rising from our garden in Ogoja, when the rains drummed down on the roof of the house and made blood-colored streams zigzag over the crackled ground. I can even hear, over the throb of automobiles jammed in an avenue, the gentle and hushed music of the Aiya River.

I can hear the voices of children shouting, they are calling to me, they're in front of the hedge at the entrance to the garden, they've brought their pebbles and their sheep vertebrae to play, to take me on a garter snake hunt. In the afternoon, after the arithmetic lesson with my mother, I'll sit down on the cement of the veranda, before the oven of the white sky to make clay gods and bake them in the sun. I remember each one of them, their names, their raised arms, their masks. Alasi, the god of thunder, Ngu, Eke-Ifite the mother goddess, Agwu the prankster. But there are many more, every day I make up a new name, they are my *chis*, the spirits that protect me and intercede with God on my behalf.

I'll watch the fever rise in the twilit sky, the lightning snake silently between the scales of gray clouds wreathed in fire. When the night has grown black, I'll listen to the steps of the thunder slowly approaching, the swell that makes my hammock rock and blows on the flame of my lamp. I'll listen to my mother's voice counting the seconds that separate us from the impact of the lightning and calculating its distance at the rate of three hundred and thirty-three meters per second. At last the wind and the extremely cold rain, moving along the crowns of the trees with all of its might; I can hear each branch groan and crack, the air in the room fills with the dust stirred up by the rain as it hits the ground.

It is all so far away, so close. A simple partition as thin as a mirror separates the world of today and that of yesterday. I'm not speaking of nostalgia. That dereistic affliction has never been a source of pleasure for me. I'm speaking of substance, of sensations, of the most logical part of my life.

Something was given to me, something was taken away from me. That which is definitively absent from my childhood: having had a father, having grown up by his side in the comfort of the family circle. I know, with no regrets or extraordinary illusions, that I lacked that. When a man watches the light on the face of the woman he loves day after day, when he tries to catch every sly glimmer in his child's eye. All of the things that can never be captured in any portrait or photograph.

But I remember everything I received when I arrived in Africa for the first time: such intense freedom that it burned inside of me, inebriated me, gave me so much pleasure it was painful.

I don't mean to speak of exoticism: children are absolute strangers to that vice. Not because they see through beings and objects, but precisely because they see nothing but them: to me a tree, a hollow in the land, a column of carpenter ants, a band of turbulent kids looking for a game, an old man with blurry eyes holding out an emaciated hand, a street in an African village on market day, were every street in every village, every old man, every child, every tree, and every ant. That treasure is still alive deep within me, it cannot be eradicated. Much more than simple memories, it is made up of basic truths.

If I had not experienced that carnal knowledge of Africa, if I had not inherited the part of my life before my birth, what would I have become?

Today I'm alive, I travel, I have in turn founded a family, I have taken root in other places. Yet at all times, like an ethereal substance floating between the partitions of reality, I am traversed by those days of old in Ogoja. In waves, it floods over me, and leaves me in a daze. Not only that childhood memory, extraordinarily precise with regard to all the sensations, the odors, the tastes, the impression of relief and empty spaces, the sensation of duration.

It is in writing it down that I now understand. That memory is not mine alone. It is also the memory of the time that preceded my birth, when my mother and father walked together on the highland trails, in the kingdoms of western Cameroon. The memory of my father's hopes and fears, his loneliness, his distress in Ogoja. The memory of moments of happiness, when my mother and father are united in love that they believe to be eternal. Back then, they walked freely on the trails and the names of places penetrated me like family names, Bali, Nkom, Bamenda, Banso, Nkong-samba, Revi, Kwaja. And the names of lands, Mbembé, Kaka, Nsungli, Bum, Fungom. The high plateaus where the herds of cattle with moon-shaped horns snagging the clouds move slowly forward between Lassim and Ngonzin.

Perhaps in the end, my old dream wasn't wrong. Though my father became the African by force of destiny, today I think I can truly believe in the existence of my African mother, the one who embraced and nourished me at the moment of my conception, the moment of my birth.

DECEMBER 2003–JANUARY 2004

A NOTE ON THE TYPE

THE AFRICAN *has been set in Minion, a type designed by Robert Slimbach in 1990. An offshoot of the designer's researches during the development of Adobe Garamond, Minion hybridized the characteristics of numerous Renaissance sources into a single calligraphic hand. Unlike many early faces developed exclusively for digital typesetting, drawings for Minion were transferred to the computer early in the design phase, preserving much of the freshness of the original concept. Conceived with an eye toward overall harmony, Minion's capitals, lowercase letters, and numerals were carefully balanced to maintain a well-groomed "family" appearance – both between roman and italic and across the full range of weights. A decidedly contemporary face, Minion makes free use of the qualities Slimbach found most appealing in the types of the fifteenth and sixteenth centuries. Crisp drawing and a narrow set width make Minion an economical and easygoing book type, and even its name evokes its adaptable, affable, and almost self-effacing nature, referring as it does to a small size of type, a faithful or favored servant, and a kind of peach.*

DESIGN & COMPOSITION BY CARL W. SCARBROUGH